A Rose Amongst Thorns

SEMONE DEON KING

ISBN 978-1-964462-59-2 (Paperback)
ISBN 978-1-964462-60-8 (Ebook)

Inquiries and Book Orders should be addressed to:

Leavitt Peak Press
17901 Pioneer Blvd Ste L #298, Artesia, California 90701
Phone #: 2092191548

I DEDICATE THIS BOOK TO MY three children: Phil Junior, Timothy, and Ethan.

No matter what I've been going through in my life, Phil Junior has always been there for me offering support. When I was in trouble, he did not hesitate to drop everything to be by my side at what proved to be one of the most difficult times in my life.

Timothy has always been there, advising me through some very difficult situations. He has always offered not just emotional support, but financial support throughout. No matter what I have gone through, Timothy has remained constant. No matter how much pressure he has been put under, he has always come through for me.

Ethan has been my shoulder to cry on. He has been right there going through most of the things I have been through right along with me. Ethan has been my strength. He has been my rock. Although Ethan is the youngest of my children, he has been through the most drama. He is very young; he is wise way beyond his years. He has lived through a lifetime of misery in his short life – more than most people live through in their entire lives. There are people who are jealous of Ethan, but believe me; they could not walk a day in his shoes. I would like to think that the things Ethan has been through have made him the wonderful young man that he is today.

I am so blessed to have three wonderful children.

MY BIRTH

I AM EVERY WOMAN! THROUGHOUT THIS journey called life I have been at the top, I have been in the middle, and I have been at the very bottom. Just as a queen has to be able to relate to her dignitaries at the highest level, whilst being able to relate to hardworking middle class people, she also has to be able to relate to the homeless person or the beggar in the street! I am every woman! This is the true story of my life to date.

In the early winter of October 1959, I was born Semone Deon King to Elizabeth Deon King and Gerald Simms in the country of Jamaica, West Indies. Sit back, definitely fasten your seatbelt, and let me tell you about my life.

My mother's name is Elizabeth Deon King. She was, by profession, a dressmaker. These days we would refer to her as a seamstress, and she loved to sew. Elizabeth could also do embroidery by hand. Her work was just so beautiful to look at, and she was very skilled at dressmaking. She could go to the store and look in the window at a dress, and then come home and make the identical dress. She was able to make a good living from her skills, but she chose to do other things instead. Elizabeth was five feet seven inches tall. She was heavyset, approximately twenty stones in weight (280 pounds); light skinned; and had long, thick, black hair and brown eyes. She was an attractive-looking woman who, at the time of my birth, was twenty years old. I was Elizabeth's second child. I had a brother, James, who was two years my senior.

In the West Indies in those days there were seers, who were practitioners of the Obeah religion, a religion that, in today's society, is more commonly known as witchcraft. One of the seer's roles was to predict certain events in people's lives; for example, to foretell if a pregnant woman would deliver normally or if there would be complications. People were so afraid that they treated whatever the seer told them as the truth. And they were so obedient that they followed everything they were told in detail. The people were of the opinion that, if they did not follow what the seer told them, then some sort of harm would come upon them or their families. Prior to my birth, my mother, Elizabeth, and my grandmother, Suzanna King, as was customary in those days, went to consult with a seer. The seer gave them some terrible news. Elizabeth and Suzanna were told that I would be stillborn. They were rigid with fear, as in the past, the seer's predictions had often come to pass.

The seer did offer Elizabeth and Suzanna a glimmer of hope, as there was a treatment that he was able to carry out that would save my life. This would consist of some sort of witchcraft. This treatment, however, was very expensive, and neither Suzanna nor Elizabeth could afford to pay for it. Elizabeth, at this time, was seven months pregnant, so time was of the essence. She and Suzanna started asking family members and friends if they were able to help with some monetary donations, but no one seemed to be able to offer any money to help. Elizabeth and Suzanna were in a huge dilemma, and they felt trapped. Time was running out, although Elizabeth counted as a bonus every day that passed during which she could still feel me moving around in her belly. This proved to be very comforting for both of them. Eventually they gave up trying to raise the money, because they realized it would be impossible to raise such a large sum of money in such a short period of time. They resigned themselves to the fact that I would be stillborn. As my birth drew nearer, Elizabeth got more and more despondent. She did not want to eat or drink. She felt there was no point. But the one thing that kept her going each day was that she could still feel me moving around in her belly.

Our community was very small, so word spread very quickly about my impending birth. In this community there was only one midwife. Having heard the prediction of the seer concerning my birth, everyone knew that the midwife would not attend my birth. As the midwife was responsible for each birth, if there was a negative report from the seer, the midwife would not attend the birth. This was a common practice, although it was not actually said out loud among the people. The midwife would not knowingly take on the responsibility of a birth that was predicted to go badly; a stillbirth would reflect badly on her reputation.

In those days, in small communities, it was customary for the midwife to visit the mothers to be and get acquainted with them before the birth. If the pregnancy was not considered high risk, then the midwife would deliver the baby at the mother's home. Hospital births in those days were very rare. Generally, because everyone lived fairly close together, a family member of the mother to be would be nominated to go to the midwife's home when the mother to be went into labour. The midwife would then gather what she needed and make her way to the mother's home immediately. There were no telephones in those days either, so information had to be relayed in person.

It was no surprise, therefore, that when Elizabeth went into labour and sent for the midwife, the midwife did not attend my birth. The midwife was requested three times, and each time the she had an excuse as to why she was unable to attend. At the third request, however, the midwife was told that a healthy baby had been delivered, and her assistance was now required. Only after hearing this did the midwife attend my birth. I was born a beautiful, healthy baby girl. The delivery was normal and quite uneventful.

From that day on, I grew and developed but was quite sickly. I would get high temperatures and colds constantly. In those days it was customary for the doctor to give injections as a form of medication. When I was two years old, however, the doctor informed Elizabeth that, because I had already received so many injections, my body was no longer responding to the medicine. I had developed immunity. By age two I had already had seventy injections. Elizabeth, Suzanna, and the rest of my family were very distraught because without the injections I would die. I was constantly ill, and my immune system seemed unable to fight any infections, so as time went on, I regressed from a normal toddler to a baby again. I could no longer walk or talk. I had lost a lot of weight because I was unable to eat or drink normal food. I was eating only baby food.

Seemingly, I was dying. My mother had given up on me, as all I would do each and every day was cry and cry, and when I wasn't crying, I would just lie in the bed and make low moaning noises. There were only two people who never gave up on me – my grandmother, Suzanna, and my Uncle Samuel. Samuel would come and pick me up and try to comfort me. Suzanna would yell, 'Pick up that child, Elizabeth! She is not yet dead!'

Elizabeth was in a state of depression and had gotten to the point where she could not stand to see me suffering each day; she just wished that I would hurry up and die!

A Stranger in Town

OURS WAS A VERY SMALL district, which meant that everyone knew each other and also their families, so whenever a stranger came into town it was a big thing. My family owned a corner shop that served the villagers, as the next shop was in town, which was some distance away. One day, a man showed up in the shop. For now we will call him Matthew, as Elizabeth did not know his name then, and still doesn't today. Matthew was approximately six foot two. He had a medium build; curly, black hair; pretty, white teeth; and a beautiful smile. He was very attractive to look at. He was dark skinned and very athletic looking. As Matthew walked in, he noticed me in the back room of the shop in my bed, as the door between the shop and the room was open. This was pretty much how I spent my days back then. Elizabeth would be in the shop with the door open, so she could keep an eye on me.

Matthew commented to Elizabeth what a beautiful child I was, and Elizabeth just broke down and started crying, explaining to him that I was dying, and that she was just waiting for that to happen, as the doctors had given up on me. At this point, something strange happened to Elizabeth. She experienced a feeling she could not explain, but she just felt herself wanting to trust Matthew, a total stranger. Somehow, she felt safe with him, so when Matthew asked her, 'If I told you to do something that would help your daughter, would you trust me to do it?' Elizabeth found herself saying yes; after all, she reasoned with herself, she had nothing to lose! I was already dying!

Matthew then asked Elizabeth to hand him a bottle of Guinness stout from the shelf, and Elizabeth complied. Matthew opened the bottle, and he then proceeded to go outside of the shop. He poured half of the stout into the ground whilst muttering words in a strange language that Elizabeth did not understand; indeed, she had never heard it before. He then came back into the shop and gave the half-empty bottle back to Elizabeth. Finally, Matthew gave Elizabeth strict instructions to follow. He told her the names of three herbs. She was to boil these herbs in water and add the herbs and water to the Guinness in the bottle until the bottle was full. His instructions got even stranger. After she filled the bottle back up with the ingredients, she was to bury the bottle in the ground for three days. On the third day, she was to remove the bottle and give me one teaspoonful three times per day.

Elizabeth informed Suzanna of this strange man and told her about the peace that she also felt about what Matthew had asked her to do. Elizabeth and Suzanna decided that, as there was no other hope for me, they would do as Matthew had instructed. Elizabeth carried out Matthew's instructions, and they anxiously waited for the third day. After all, again, what did they have to lose? Three days at this time seemed like three years to Elizabeth. The third day finally came, and Elizabeth dug up the bottle and gave me one teaspoon of the liquid as instructed by Matthew. Throughout the day, she gave me two more doses. Elizabeth and Suzanna became very frightened, because all I did that first day and night was just sleep. Elizabeth got so frightened she would try to wake me up periodically just to make sure I was still alive.

The following morning, however, I woke up and spoke the first words I had spoken in months: 'Mama, me want milk.' Those words were like music to everyone's ears. From that day, as a child, I was never ill again.

I know you are wondering what happened to Matthew. Surely Elizabeth would have liked to thank him for saving her child's life! Well, you guessed it. As suddenly as Matthew had appeared, he also disappeared. In fact, as soon as Matthew gave the bottle to Elizabeth along with the instructions, Elizabeth turned to put the bottle on the counter behind her. When she turned around again, Matthew had disappeared. Elizabeth got up and walked outside the shop and looked as far as her eyes could see in all directions, but Matthew was nowhere to be seen. Elizabeth asked all around the village if anyone else had seen Matthew. Not one other person reported having seen Matthew then or afterwards. An angel here on earth? What do you think? I'm living proof!

A New Chapter in My Life

Elizabeth had twelve children in all. Three died. Twins were stillborn when Elizabeth got into a fight when she was eight months pregnant and lost both babies. Another child, a little girl, was with us for only three days. She was born healthy and so beautiful with a mop of straight, black hair. Elizabeth named her Adora, and she certainly was adorable. I was six years old when Adora was born and died, but I have never forgotten her.

My brother James was the eldest. I followed. Then came a brother, Zavier; another brother, Luke; a sister, Angel; another sister, Hyacinth; yet another sister, Claudia; then a brother, Roger; followed by, last but not least, a sister, April.

My big brother James and I had such fun growing up; that is, until he was sent away to his dad when he was ten years old. I felt as if my other half had gone missing. We were so close, then one day I woke up, and he was gone. I was confused. I thought I had done something to make James go away. I felt as if my whole world had collapsed. Elizabeth never offered me any explanation.

I never saw James again until I was twenty years old when I met up with him in England. I still felt so close to him. We recalled a few childhood memories, some of which were pleasant and some of which were very unpleasant. One such unpleasant memory was the night Angel was conceived. James and I shared a bedroom with Elizabeth at the time, and James and I also shared a bed. James and I were in our bed fast asleep, and we were awakened to some strange noises. James and I started doing what kids do – we started giggling, and as we did so, we heard Elizabeth call out our names. We promptly pretended we were sleeping. Elizabeth, satisfied I guess that we were asleep because we did not answer her, resumed her activities, but James and I were both traumatized. James and I never spoke of this as children until the day we met up again when I was twenty and he was twenty-two years old. On that long-ago night we had known not to answer Elizabeth when she called out our names, because we were both petrified that we were going to get a beating. The next morning, James and I thought it was Christmas, because it seemed that a lot of money had fallen onto the floor from the pockets of the man who would become Angel's dad. James and I had great fun picking up all the coins. Of course we were not allowed to keep it. James and I never saw Angel's dad, because he always came at night while we were supposedly asleep, and he would be gone when we woke up in the morning. James and I always knew when Angel's dad came around, because he always left coins on the floor. I later learned that the coins fell from his money apron, as he had a mobile shop and would still be wearing his apron when he came around. I think that, when we met as adults, James and I just really wanted to see if either one remembered the incident, and we sure did – in great detail. Of course, as children, we had no idea what was going on, but as we grew up, we connected the dots and realized what those noises were. At the time of this incident, I believe James was about nine years old and I was seven.

James and I had a good time catching up and met up several times afterwards to go out for meals and so forth. I met James's dad and his stepmother. I also met his father's wife's children. James's dad, James Senior, did not have any other children; James was his only child.

James seemed very happy, and women were the love of his life. At any given time, James was in love with at least two women at the same time, and he genuinely loved them both.

As a child growing up, I did not know I had a brother called Zavier. I didn't meet him until I was thirty-six years old. Elizabeth had given him away as a baby! As a result of this, Zavier did not go to school until he was fourteen years old, because the family he was given to sent their own children to school, but they expected Zavier to stay at home and cook and clean; he was not sent to school with the other children in the family. Elizabeth found out about this somehow, and took Zavier away from the family, but I still did not know anything about Zavier's existence. Zavier is a very handsome young man, about six foot four with light skin. He is very much a ladies' man. He is married and has a family of his own.

I look at Zavier and I ask myself the question: How could Elizabeth give away her beautiful son? He is gorgeous! How could she? Zavier is scarred by this experience, and even now that he is a grown man, his hurt and pain shows through when he speaks on this subject. Zavier holds no malice, however, and I am so proud of him. I love him so much. He is by far my favourite sibling!

Luke follows Zavier. He is stocky and about five foot nine inches with light skin and hazel eyes. He is quite handsome. Luke is very quiet, but very sneaky. He behaves as if he is so good, but he is a snake in the grass. Luke has the ability to make you trust him and to make you feel so safe around him, but in reality all he's doing is setting you up for a fall. Probably luckily, Luke never got married. He does have two children with two different mothers. Despite his character, I love Luke dearly.

Angel follows Luke. I love my sister Angel. She is eight years younger than I, and we were very close growing up until I was sent away when I was sixteen years old. Angel has always been heavy; even as a child growing up, she was adorable. Angel is approximately sixteen stone (225 pounds), five foot nine inches, and is quite a pretty woman. She has brown eyes and short, thick, black hair.

I remember as a child growing up, it was a treat to get new clothes, and when I did get something new, I would treasure it. One such item was a beautiful blouse Elizabeth bought me. One day I came home from school to find Angel wearing my brand-new blouse. I told her I was not happy about it. In fact, I was so angry I started to cry. Elizabeth found out about this, and she proceeded to give me the beating of my life, cursing me whilst beating me, telling me how selfish I was that I did not want to share my clothes with my sister. She called me some terrible names. As a child, I was greatly impacted by this experience. To this day, I will not lend my clothes or share my clothes with anyone. If someone wants to borrow my clothes, I happily give her whatever she wants and tell her to keep it. Angel has four children, three girls and a boy.

Angel was followed by Hyacinth. Hyacinth is five foot eleven inches, light skinned, slim, and very beautiful. She is a very jealous, very shallow, and a very selfish person. She does not want anyone to have anything better than what she has. She pretends to be a friend to see what she is able to take from people, and how she can use people to benefit her, and when she has taken what she wants from them, she treats them as if they never existed. She will happily curse people out in a heartbeat without ever saying she is sorry, even when she is wrong. Needless to say, she never got married, as whenever any man got close to her, he would see her for what she is and run a mile. She has one child. She is by far my least favourite sibling!

Hyacinth is followed by Claudia. Claudia is approximately five foot seven inches, light skinned, and slim to medium in build. She weighs about twelve stone (168 pounds) and keeps herself in good condition. She is married to a lovely man. She has two children, a boy and a girl, who do not belong to her husband. She had those children before she met him. I like Claudia. she is a nice person, but is very easily influenced by others. She does not have the backbone to stand up for what she knows is right, and she just goes along with the crowd.

Claudia is followed by Roger. Roger is approximately six foot five inches and light skinned. He is very arrogant. He is a handsome man, and he knows it and uses his looks to influence situations. He is definitely not a gentleman. He will ensure that other people spend every last penny that they have, whilst his hand will not go into his pocket. He is married to a beautiful lady, and they have one child. Oh, how I feel so sorry for her.

Last, but not least, is April. April is approximately five foot nine inches. She is heavyset, weighing around sixteen stone (224 pounds). She is married to a Caucasian man, and they have three children together. April is the meanest and the nastiest person I have ever had the displeasure of meeting in my life. She will scheme behind peo-ple's backs, and set them up so she can steal every penny they have, whilst all the time pretending to have their best interest at heart. She is a scary person to know – pure evil.

All of my siblings have different fathers, so to me, meeting them and getting along with them is just like going out and meeting different people from other families. They all have different characters, some of which are good, and some of which are bad. There is absolutely nothing called loyalty among them. They will sell you out in a heartbeat. There is a saying: you can choose your friends, but you cannot choose your family. This is certainly true.

GROWING UP IN JAMAICA

M Y FAMILY WAS VERY POOR when I was growing up in Jamaica. There were times when we would eat steamed crackers for dinner and be happy that we had even that. How do you steam crackers? Well, you put a bit of butter or margarine on some water crackers, which are plain crackers, fairly thick and hard. In our case, sometimes we didn't even have butter or margarine. Then you put the crackers in a saucepan with a tiny bit of water. Cover the pot, put it over heat, and let the crackers steam! Try it. It's delicious! Jamaican crackers.

Whenever Elizabeth cooked rice, all the children would fight over whose turn it was to eat the rice at the bottom of the pot, because it was usually burnt a little, which made it crispy, and oh how I loved that burnt rice! The only meat I knew growing up was chicken back – you know, the bony part of the chicken, which most people throw away these days. Whenever we had chicken back, we felt privileged. Most days our main dish would be a leafy vegetable called *callaloo*, and we would have that with salted codfish. That was our meat. We would have this sometimes with rice or green bananas, dumplings, and yams. For breakfast we would have porridge. This was pretty much our diet. On some Sunday mornings for breakfast we would have chocolate tea, fried dumplings, and callaloo and saltfish, or, sometimes we would have a fruit called *ackee* along with saltfish and fried dumplings.

Believe it or not, I was very fortunate growing up as a child in Jamaica, because I had a toy. Yes, I actually had a toy. During my entire childhood, I had only one toy. It was a doll – a white doll with big, brown eyes and long eyelashes and long blonde hair. I loved that doll. My grandma and my mother had bought it for me as a Christmas present when I was about six years old. Oh, how I cherished that doll. I treated that doll as if it was made of eggs. I never damaged her. I kept her until I was sixteen years old, and then I gave her to my sister Hyacinth when I was leaving Jamaica. It was a bit worse for wear by then, as I'd had it for ten years. The hair was mostly gone, but I didn't care. I still cherished her. That doll was my best friend. It was as if that doll would come alive and listen to all my problems that I wasn't able to tell anyone else about. I would pretend I was talking to a real person. That doll kept me from going insane.

I grew up seeing Elizabeth meeting with many different men, although she was married. Elizabeth's husband, Tom, was approximately six foot four inches tall. He had light skin and hazel eyes. He was very handsome. Of course, I was very young, so I did not have a clue what was going on.

Elizabeth would send me to visit different men at their places of work or their homes to pick up money – always to pick up money. One such man was Mr Brown, a big man about six feet in height and heavyset. The moment I got into his house, he tried to have sex with me, but I was a virgin, so he was unable to penetrate me. At the time, I did not even know what he was doing. I was only thirteen years old, and sex education was not taught in school. Another man she sent me to was a burly white man, Mr Zoo. He had a big belly like a pregnant woman about to deliver. He was approximately five foot ten and heavyset. My mother sent me to his place of business, and he too tried to have sex with me. The moment I got into Mr Zoo's office, he sat in the chair and told me to sit in his lap. I was thirteen years old and had been brought up to do as I was told, particularly by adults. I was so afraid that Mr Zoo would tell Elizabeth that I had been rude to him, I did as I was instructed. Mr Zoo slipped my knickers to the side with his fingers and tried to have sex with me, but he could not penetrate me, because I was still a virgin.

I found the behaviour of these men very stressful and disgusting, never mind the fact that they were hurting me. I felt all dirty and violated, but I never told Elizabeth, because these men told me not to tell her, and besides I was very scared. Elizabeth was so strict I thought I was going to get the beating of my life, so I kept my mouth shut. I did, however, beg her not to send me back to these men. Elizabeth never once asked me why I did not want to go back; she just looked at me with that look that said, 'Shut up or else.' If you are of West Indian heritage, then you will know about that look. My pleas fell on deaf ears.

The next man Elizabeth sent me to was a big, ugly, very-dark-skinned man called Mr Nash. Mr Nash was about five foot ten inches tall, and stocky. He came around to our house quite often; in fact, Mr Nash was the only one of these men who came to our house. He was always buying me things such as material to make dresses, and he was always giving me money, which I would give straight to Elizabeth.

As I look back at this now that I am grown, I ask myself the question: Why did Elizabeth never question why Mr Nash was always giving me money? Why did she never question why he was always buying me things? Why did she not question why Mr Nash, a grown man, wanted to hang around her thirteen-year-old daughter? Why was he showing such interest in her thirteen-year-old daughter? Even though her daughter was constantly begging her not to send her to his house, and knowing the relationship she herself had with these men, did it not ever cross her mind that those men would be molesting her daughter?

Mr Nash picked me up from school on several occasions on his bike. Oh, how I hated it! The kids in school would tease me relentlessly. Elizabeth did not mind Mr Nash picking me up and taking me places, but I hated it. Soon Elizabeth was sending me to his house regularly every Friday evening to pick up money. It was not long before he started touching me inappropriately. The first day he assaulted me, he went to a drawer in his kitchen and he took out a big knife. He held it up real close to my face, and he said, 'See this knife? If you tell your mother, or anyone else what I'm doing to you, I'm going to kill your mother and all your sisters and brothers.'

On one occasion I pretended to sleep when he started his moles-tation, and to my surprise he left me alone. I then thought to myself, *If I pretend to be asleep every time Elizabeth sends me to his house, then Mr Nash would not touch me.* But that did not work. It was not long before I would feel him lifting up my dress and pulling at my panties. He would use his fingers and Vaseline each time I went to his house.

I begged Elizabeth not to send me back there. Each time I would come home crying and shaking, but she just ignored me. Now if you are bought up with West Indian parents, you know that, unless you wanted your teeth on the floor, you did as you were told and liked it!

This went on for some time, and one Friday evening, Mr Nash was assaulting me, and he suddenly stopped. I was so relieved, as I was in great pain. I did not realize why he had stopped until I was on my way home. In those days there were no public toilets, so, if you wanted to relieve yourself, you would just find a spot in the bushes and hide where you could not be seen. This Friday evening I was in pain, so I stopped to wee in the bushes, and there was blood in my urine. I was so scared, but I could not tell anyone, because Mr Nash had long ago made sure I wouldn't. I was afraid of him, and afraid for my health, and I was only thirteen years old.

THE RAPE

MR NASH AGAIN ASKED ELIZABETH if he could pick me up from school and take me to his house in the country. Elizabeth again agreed – to my horror. 'Please don't send me, Mom,' I begged, but my pleas fell on deaf ears. Mr Nash picked me up from school and took me to his house the following Friday. As soon as we got through the door, he told me, 'Take off your clothes.' I refused, and I crossed my hands as if hugging myself, but I was clutching my dress at the neck. He grabbed my dress and ripped it, and yelled at me to take it off. I stood there terrified in my bra and knickers, with my hands crossed against my chest, trying to hide my breasts. 'Take off your bra!' he yelled. I didn't. I just stood there frozen to the spot trying to cover myself by bending in the foetal position. He grabbed at my bra, and I struggled with him to hold on to it. Finally he ripped it and again yelled at me to take it off. Terrified, I did as I was told.

Mr Nash then came right up to my face. He was so close he was almost touching my face with his, and he looked me straight in the eyes and told me very chillingly, 'You can scream as loud as you like. *No one will hear you!*' He had built a house way out in the woods. There were no other houses around for miles. Mr Nash then proceeded to push me onto the bed. I screamed at the top of my lungs whilst he brutally raped me, taking my virginity!

When it was over, he sewed up my dress and bra and took me home to my mother. I was bleeding and could hardly walk. I spent what seemed like weeks in the shower. I would shower in cold water, trying to dull the pain of my wounded vagina. I would then take myself to bed still in pain and still bleeding, knowing that I couldn't tell my mother what this man – *her friend* – had done to me.

As if this wasn't enough, there was more humiliation in store for me! My family were Seventh Day Adventists, so the next day, being Saturday, was church day. The brutality of the rape had started my periods, so not only did I have to deal with the rape, I also had to endure starting my periods for the first time in this savage way. I thought I was dying. There was no sex education in school, so in my mind I still thought babies came from the sky. You see, when I asked my mother where she got the baby from that she'd recently had, she said, 'See that aeroplane up there in the sky?' I looked up. Elizabeth told me that the plane had brought her the baby! I, of course, believed her. Why wouldn't I? I did not know any better at the time!

Again, being of West Indian parents, I did as I was told, so I was not allowed to choose the clothes I wore. Even when I was thirteen, my mother would pick out the clothes that she wanted me to wear. Her logic was that, if she bought them, she could choose them. She would lay my clothes out on the bed, and her choices were not open for debate. I wore whatever she laid out for me. Yep, you guessed it. On that Saturday, Elizabeth picked out a beautiful *white* dress for me to wear, and of course, I had no say in the matter. On top of that, I had to walk a mile and a half to church.

To make matters even worse, Elizabeth was not going to church that day; she was not feeling well. So I was going with her friend, Mrs Jones, who was my best friend's mother. The journey to church was uneventful. When I got to church, I tried to sit on the edge of the bench and not sit on my nice white dress, but that didn't work. The very kind lady behind us whispered to Mrs Jones that I had blood on my dress. Mrs Jones took me outside and asked me, 'Do you know what this is?' I held my head down looking at the ground, as I thought she knew what had happened to me, so I shivered as I said no. Mrs Jones got a pin and pinned up my dress and told me, 'Go home to your mother. She will explain to you what this is.'

I was petrified. I went home and told Elizabeth what Mrs Jones had said. She told me it was my period and that I was now a woman (hmm … if only she knew!). She told me I would get a period every month. I could no longer use anybody else's soap or washcloth. She gave me a bottle of Dettol liquid antiseptic and disinfectant and some sanitary towels, and told me how to take care of myself. Elizabeth then said, 'You are a bit young to start on your periods. Did anybody trouble you?' Oh, I wanted to tell her so badly what had happened to me, but I just got a flashback of Mr Nash showing me the knife and telling me how he would use it on my family if I told anyone, so I just said no. Elizabeth said, 'Are you sure?' And I just said, 'Yes, I'm sure.' I quickly walked away, the tears welling up in my eyes.

The years went by, and since the day I was raped, I have never seen Mr Nash again. I constantly lived in fear that one day he would show up again, and do to me again what he had done before, but thankfully this did not happen. Did it not strike Elizabeth as strange that Mr Nash never showed up anymore? Elizabeth never sent me to his house anymore to pick up money either.

When something bad happens to you in your life, there are two ways to look at it. One, you can learn from it and allow it to make you better, or two, you can wallow in self-pity and allow the incident to make you bitter! When I was raped as a young child and was unable to talk about it with my mother, as I was so terrified of being beaten, I made the decision that, when I grew up and had children, I would make sure that they would be able to come to me and talk to me about anything and everything!

I have seen many people who have gone through a rape. Some have become promiscuous or have behaved in other self-destructive ways, and they have blamed their behaviour on the fact that they were raped. Everyone handles rape differently, but I am a firm believer that whatever victims do, they shouldn't live their lives as victims, because then the rapists wins! If something like this happens to you, stay focused gather strength from the situation, learn from it, and allow it to propel you forward. I know this is easier said than done, but I know that this can be done, because I am living proof. Even as a child, I was able to follow this advice.

I decided to include this chapter of my life in this book because I am hoping to encourage any readers who might be in a dark place right now because of a rape, or any other kind of violence. I am here to tell them that this too shall pass! God has a plan for your life just as he had a plan for my life. Many times, I have asked the

Lord, 'Why did this have to happen to me? Why was my virginity stolen from me at such a young age? The Lord revealed to me that I had to go through the experience because today, my survival and my victory are my testimony. This is my destiny! Don't allow a rape or other violence to take away your hopes and your dreams. There is life beyond violence. Allow the experience to make you wiser and stronger and to be able to encourage someone else along the way who may be suffering.

Life Goes on After Rape

FOR THREE YEARS AFTER THE rape, my life was pretty uneventful. I started attending a different high school. This was a private school, which Elizabeth paid for each term. Elizabeth did not want to pay to send me to this school, but because I did not pass the eleven plus exam in Jamaica, I could not go to one of the better schools. I felt so dumb for not passing this exam. I felt so much pressure from Elizabeth. I remember looking in the newspaper for my name, and it was not there. And I remember looking across and putting two names together to make it into my name. I felt useless at the time. Elizabeth made me feel so ashamed and dumb. Sending me to the private school was more for Elizabeth's benefit, as she was able to tell her friends that I was going to a private school. I really did not particularly care where I went to school so long as I went. I was not able to stay there for long, as Elizabeth was not able to continue to pay the school fees, so I went to a public school later on.

Elizabeth was still married, but nothing had changed on that front. She was still being promiscuous with several different men, but I was asked to go and collect money from only one man, Mr McMillan, and it happened every Friday evening. Why Friday evenings? This is when the men would be paid. Mr McMillan would be at work when I went to see him, so I would go to the gate of his workplace. He would meet me and give me the money, and I would be on my way. I was not allowed to go inside his workplace, as he worked with dangerous chemicals. That suited me just fine considering the alternatives. Mr McMillan was a kind, gentle man, so I was very sorry when Elizabeth told me that I would no longer be going to collect from him on a Friday evening. He had an accident at work, and was burnt very badly. He was a black man, about six foot four with light skin. He always spoke nicely to me. He actually looked very much like Elizabeth's husband.

Elizabeth, on the other hand, was very mean to me. As a child growing up, I felt no love from Elizabeth. She never once hugged me or told me that she loved me. I did not know how it felt to be told that I was loved by my mother or to be held by my mother. The only thing Elizabeth told me was that I was a dirty John Crow, which is what we call turkey vultures in the West Indies. It is a black bird, the scavenger of the earth. She told me that, when I grew up, not even a dog would drink water from me because I was so nasty. I felt like a slave. I had go down on my knees to shine the floor with a brush that was made from dried coconut. Elizabeth's favourite words were, 'I want to be able to see my face in that floor.' I had to take care of all my brothers and sisters, because I was the first girl child and the second eldest child. My brother James, who was the eldest child, had been long gone since he was ten years old. Oh how I missed James. I do sometimes wonder, if James had still been at home, would I have been raped? Because maybe Elizabeth would have sent James to these men instead of me! I had no communication with James, and I don't think that Elizabeth had much either.

When I was a child growing up, Elizabeth was very strict, and I was not allowed to speak to boys. It was as if they were a different species to me. As a result, I grew up not really knowing how to have a conversation with a man. Elizabeth's husband did not like me, so he never spoke to me except to curse me and call me some ugly names; for example, he would refer to me as the 'lean side gal' rather than call me by my name.

I have often wondered what it would be like to have a dad – someone to call me his princess and to hold me and tell me that he loved me. Elizabeth told me that, when she was five months pregnant with me, my father died of malaria fever. My lack of a father figure gave me such a complex as I grew up, because I just did not know how to relate to a man. My self-esteem as a child was so low, although I did not know it at the time. Whenever I walked on the street, I would never look anyone in the eyes; I would walk with my head held down. I felt so ugly. I had no one to talk to, as my beloved

Grandma was living far away from Elizabeth, and so I was unable to communicate with her except on special occasions like birthdays or Christmas, when we would all come together as a family. In those days, there were no telephones in the houses in the country. Apart from these holidays, I did not get to see my grandmother.

I grew up a lonely little girl, even though I was in a household with four other children. Yes, even though there were nine children of us left, I did not grow up with the rest of my siblings. The others grew up with my grandmother and with some other people. The only siblings I grew up with were the four children Elizabeth had with Tom. I was so lonely. I had only one friend that Elizabeth would allow me to speak to. Clara was my best and only friend. She was the daughter of my mother's friend – the one who took me to church the day after the rape. Clara had brothers, but I was not allowed so speak to them except to say hello, and that would be the end of our conversation.

MY NEW JOURNEY

J ust when I turned sixteen, my mother announced that she
was sending me to England. You need to understand that I was
not asked if I wanted to go to England. There was no discussion;
I was told that I was going, no questions asked. Elizabeth told me
that she had a very distant cousin by the name of Gerald who lived
in England. Gerald had agreed that I could come over and stay with
him and his family. Elizabeth did not want her husband, Tom, to
know that she was sending me away, so she arranged everything in
secret, and it was not until the day I was leaving that she told Tom
about my departure. Tom was very surprised and just turned and
walked away. I guess he was glad to see the back of me. He hated me.
I was not his child. I never saw Tom again after I left Jamaica.

Elizabeth took me to the airport. During the journey, I was
very sad in my heart, but of course I had to pretend I was happy and
excited. Elizabeth thought she was doing the best thing for me. I did
not want to leave my family – my sisters, my brothers. How would I
manage without them? I was totally bewildered, and to make matters
worse, my siblings were not allowed to come to the airport, so I had
to settle for saying my goodbyes at home. The journey to the airport
seemed to take days, but in reality, it took only an hour or so. I did
not communicate much on my way there, because all I wanted to do
was to cry, but of course I couldn't.

This was my first time flying, and I did not know what to
expect. I was excited, nervous, and sad all at the same time, because
I was leaving the only family I knew. When it was time to board the
plane, I said my goodbyes to Elizabeth, but little did I know I was
now on my own! Petrified with fear, I walked the long walkway to the
plane with an air hostess. She was very nice to me. She tried to engage

me in conversation to take my mind off what was happening I guess. I was not a normal sixteen-year-old. I was very shy, very withdrawn, and although I was very intelligent, I was somehow scared to have a conversation with an adult. Growing up with Elizabeth, I had been told that, as a child, I should be seen but not heard. This of course contributed to my very low self-esteem, and I also thought nobody would be interested in anything I had to say.

Once I was on the plane, I felt so all alone. I was so tiny. I was only five foot three, and I weighed only seven stone (ninety-eight pounds). The flight was long. It seemed to take days, but of course it was only eight hours. To my surprise, they fed me food on the plane. They even gave me drinks. The air hostesses were very nice and polite to me. They actually treated me like a person. This was new to me. I was not used to being spoken to! I was used to being yelled at, followed by a barrage of insults. I liked this behaviour; it was nice. I could learn to enjoy being spoken to like a normal human being.

Normal? *Define normal*, I said to myself. Was being raped at thirteen normal? Was being afraid of your mother normal? Was living in fear of being raped again normal? Was not knowing what your father even looked like normal? Was not even knowing your father's name normal? Was getting up at five every morning to take care of your brothers and sisters normal? Was being tired constantly at age sixteen because you were overworked normal? Was being hated by your stepfather normal? Was never being hugged by your mother or told by your mother that you are loved normal? Was being sent to collect money from men every Friday evening normal? Were any of these things normal? Well, in my world, all of these things were perfectly normal. This was my life!

Elizabeth had told me that, when I got to England, her cousin Gerald would meet me at the airport, and he would take me through customs. I had no idea what Gerald looked like, and neither did Elizabeth, because she had never met Gerald or spoken to Gerald. She had only ever spoken to Gerald's mother, who was her Aunt Carol, and her aunt lived in Jamaica. Gerald was her Aunt's third son. Would Elizabeth ever learn? I beg to ask the question. How do you pack up your sixteen-year-old daughter and send her away to a far-away country to a man you have never even spoken to? Oh how I needed my mother. I was at the age in a young girl's life when she needs her mother, but yet, this was the time that my mother chose to send me away. Here I was at sixteen, being plucked from my family and being sent to a foreign country to someone neither my mother nor I knew.

For me, the journey to England on that plane was filled with excitement, uncertainty, worry, and sadness. I was excited about going to another country where I hoped I would have a better life than I did in Jamaica. I was uncertain because I did not know what was awaiting me in England. I was worried because I did not know if I would like England, the people I would be staying with, or their children. How would they respond to having me in their home? Why would they even want me in their home? What did I have to offer them? To them I was another mouth to feed. Would I like them? Would they like me? I had never even stayed over at a friend's house before, so I was totally unprepared. After all, Tom had hated me and called me mean names, and his house was the only house I had lived in. Would it be the same? How would I manage in a strange country with nobody that I knew? What would the food be like? How would I get new clothes? So much worry on my little head! Finally, I was also filled with sadness that my mother had chosen to send me away and that I would be away from everything and everyone I had been familiar with for my entire life.

I finally arrived in England. My first impression was that it was not at all how I had pictured it in my mind. You see nobody prepared me for what to expect, so I had painted my own picture! I thought there would be big houses on acres of land all over the place. In Jamaica, I had often heard it said that the streets in England are paved with gold. The first thing I did when I got to England was to look on the ground. I was very disappointed; there was no gold! They had lied! I thought the weather would be like Jamaican weather, but I was in for a shock. It was June, and temperatures were not as warm as they were in Jamaica. In fact, it felt quite cold. It was also quite overcast. There were a lot of high-rise buildings in England, which I later learned were called flats – apartments where people lived. There were different types of flats. Some flats were in high-rise blocks that could stand sixteen stories high, whilst some were like maisonettes, which were only two or three floors high. Depending on the area, some apartments were for sale, and some were for rent only. Everyone wanted a ground-floor flat because those usually came with a garden. The ground floor flats, however, were often reserved for disabled people, or for people who had young children. Generally, people did not look as happy as they did in Jamaica. Everyone seemed to be in a hurry. They were walking so fast. In Jamaica everyone seems to walk slowly; people are generally more relaxed. I did notice, however, that English people were very polite. Everyone I saw would smile at me, and I was quite taken aback at this. Why would anyone want to smile at me? Were they just laughing at me, I wondered. Lots of thoughts were going through my mind. I also noticed that people were very talkative. They would just come up to me and start talking to me. This was very strange to me. They would, for example, start talking about the weather – oh, what a beautiful day it was. In my mind, it wasn't. It was cold and dull. I also noticed that there were a lot of cars on the roads. In Jamaica, there were not so many vehicles. This was my initial perception of England.

Elizabeth had told me that Gerald was a diplomat, and he would come and get me through customs. When I arrived in England, however, there was no Gerald to get me through customs. When the immigration officer asked me how long I would be staying in England, I just said three months, not understanding that this meant that, when that three months expired, I would need to be out of the country. When I cleared customs and walked out into the airport, I didn't have a clue what to do. Suddenly I saw two ladies staring at me. One of them was holding a piece of cardboard with my name written on it. I had no idea who they were or why they were staring at me or how they knew my name. They approached me, and asked me if I was waiting for Gerald to pick me up. I said yes, and they introduced themselves as Jane, who was Gerald's wife, and Jean, who was Gerald's sister. They both seemed lovely.

Jane was approximately twenty-eight stone (392 pounds) in weight. She was about five foot ten with dark complexion and shoulder-length black hair and huge brown eyes. Jean, on the other hand, was of light complexion, approximately five foot four and of medium build. She weighed about twelve stone (168 pounds) and had hazel eyes.

They kept on asking me if I was tired, and they were really nice to me. You see, I was not used to an adult being nice to me. I was used to Elizabeth cursing and yelling at me. To be around someone who was nice to me, and who actually asked me what I wanted was all a bit of a shock to me. They actually hugged me at the airport and kissed me on the cheeks. I had never been hugged, let alone kissed on the cheeks! It felt strange. Was this normal behaviour? Was this how I was meant to be treated? It sure felt good. *If this is how folks in England behave, then I think I'm going to like it here*, I thought.

Jane and Gerald had four children, two boys and two girls. I was to live with them. It felt strange, because they were not my brothers and sisters; they were strangers to me. I did not want to seem ungrateful to them for having me in their home, so every night when I went to bed I would cry myself to sleep. I missed my family so much. This family was not the same; they were not my family. I was in a new country with people who spoke 'funny'. I could not understand them, and they certainly couldn't understand me; they thought I spoke 'funny' too. Jane took me everywhere with her. She enjoyed showing me off to her friends. I felt like a shy little girl who wrapped her hands around her mother's leg, and hid behind her mother every time Jane introduced me to someone new. Of course, I tried not to show just how shy and awkward I felt around new people, and thanks to Elizabeth, I was an expert at hiding how I really felt.

I think Jane quite enjoyed having me around. I loved being around Jane, because she treated me the way I imagined a normal mother would treat her child. Elizabeth's lack of attention to me had left me craving attention, and I just loved Jane because she treated me so nicely. Jane loved to eat. Jane would buy a big pack of cream crackers and sit and eat the whole pack in one night with different cheeses. Before long, I was a cheese connoisseur. I discovered I loved all the different cheeses Jane introduced me to. She was always complaining that I did not eat much, but I just had to get acquainted with the different foods. I was very good at cooking and cleaning up. Elizabeth had made sure of that. All I seemed to do when I was at home was to cook and clean up after my brothers and sisters.

Jane and Gerald's children were quite nice to me. They kept on teasing me about the way I spoke, and I would tease them about the way they spoke. Jonathan, their eldest son, was eleven. Joanna, their second daughter, was nine. She was followed by Mark, who was seven. Then came Jennifer, who was five years old. I could sit for hours just listening to the children speak. They sounded so proper. I did not sound proper at all.

After one month, I finally got to meet Gerald. He was not at all how I had imagined him. Gerald was approximately six foot five. He was very slim and dark skinned, and very well dressed. He had brown eyes and well-groomed, short hair. He was a total contrast to Jane. Jane had told me that he was working abroad, which was the reason he had been unable to pick me up at the airport. I soon came to realize, however, that the reason that Gerald had not been able to pick me up from the airport was that he had been detained at Her Majesty's pleasure (he was in prison). His diplomatic status had been revoked.

When Gerald came home, things began to change. I did not like the way he looked at me. I had seen that look before from Mr Nash, and I was terrified. One day when Jane was out, Gerald started telling me that he would like to have sex with me, and he made a pass at me. I freaked out and ran out of the house. As you will remember, my only contact with a man to that point was the rape I had endured, so I was petrified, and besides he was married to Jane. How could he even think of doing that? I did not know what to do, so I made a point of never being in the house with him alone. This meant that, more than ever, I went everywhere with Jane, even if she was just going downstairs to the shop. Jane became suspicious and started asking me some questions. I told her what had happened, very reluctantly, and she was none too pleased with Gerald. Gerald apologized to me and promised Jane that it would never happen again. I started to feel a bit more comfortable with Gerald over the course of the next few months, and he was true to his word; he never behaved in that manner towards me again.

After I had been in England for three months, Gerald took me to get me enrolled in college. Then he took me to the job centre to get a part-time job. The clerk asked to see my passport, as I was not a citizen of the UK. When she looked at my passport, she exclaimed in a loud voice that startled me, 'Oh my gosh! You should have been out of the country yesterday!' The penny finally dropped. The stamp in my passport indicated that I was not allowed to engage in any work during my three-month visit. Jane and Gerald had thought that meant that I had to wait three months before I could work and go to college. They had both been wrong. Three months was the length of time I had been given to stay in the country.

Gerald then applied to the Home Office explaining to them what had happened, and he requested that they allow me to stay in the country to study. The Home Office was very slow to respond to such matters, so whilst we were waiting, I was enrolled in college and started a course of study. After about a year, we finally heard back from the Home office. To my shock and horror, they denied my request! I could not stay in the country. They gave me a date and told me I'd have to exit the country by then! I was very stressed, so Gerald took me to a lawyer, and his law firm then started corresponding with the Home Office on my behalf. The first thing the lawyers were able to do was to get me an extended time to study whilst the Home Office reconsidered my case. It took the Home Office a further year to respond. They were more favourable at this time and extended my time so I could study and work in the UK. By this time, a few years had passed. I was now eighteen years old.

CHANGES ON THE HOME FRONT

THINGS ON THE HOME FRONT had not been going too well with Jane and Gerald. They had been fighting a lot, always yelling at each other and also at the children. I was a little surprised, however, one day when Jane sat me down and told me that she was moving back to Birmingham, which is where she was from originally, and that she was breaking up with Gerald. When I enquired why they were breaking up, Jane told me that Gerald had been having multiple affairs, and simply put, she had had enough. Jane explained that Gerald had even given her a disease called gonorrhea during her pregnancy with their last child, Jennifer. They had been fearful that Jennifer might have been born blind.

Again, It was time for me to be on my own. At eighteen years old, I had to find a place of my own. I had to work and study on my own. And I was in a strange country where I knew hardly anyone. I had made a few friends, however, one of whom was Jane's younger sister, Nadine. I was a year older than Nadine, but to look at us you would think Nadine was older. She was into going out to clubs, and she loved dancing and drinking. Nadine was very confident with boys. She found it very easy to talk to guys, but I was very reserved and too scared to even hold a conversation, because I didn't know how to, as I had not been allowed to talk to boys when I was younger. Elizabeth was not with me in England, but I sure felt as if she was right there watching my every move. 'Train up a child in the way he should go: and when he is old, he will not depart from it' (Proverbs 22:6 King James Version). I was eighteen years old. I had never been to the cinema. I had never been to a club of any sort. I had never had an alcoholic drink. I had never even been kissed!

Jane had now moved away, whilst Gerald stayed in the apartment that was the family's home. Although I could have carried on living at the apartment with Gerald, somehow I knew I just wouldn't feel comfortable being there alone with him. He had given me no reason since that first time not to feel safe with him, but that was still in the back of my mind. I started looking for a flat to rent, and I was very lucky to find one. I had to wait a few weeks for the landlord to carry out some maintenance work on the property.

It was at this time that, one Saturday night, I was invited out to a house party. I arrived home at five on Sunday morning, and I went directly to asleep. Not long after I went to sleep, the doorbell rang, and I heard a man saying my full name and ask Gerald if I was in. Gerald told the man that I was not there. As I listened to the conversation, I learned that these men were immigration officers; there were three of them. As soon as I heard that, I jumped out of the bed and ran and hid on the balcony of the apartment. What I did not know at the time was that there were more immigration officers downstairs, and they saw me when I ran into the balcony. They did not have a warrant at the time to search the premises, so they could not enter the apartment without Gerald's permission.

The next Saturday night, I again went out, and I came home about the same time – five o'clock Sunday morning. At exactly eight o'clock on that Sunday morning the doorbell rang. For some reason, I sat upright in bed, as if I had been compelled to do so. Again, I heard my full name being called, and this time they had come prepared with a search warrant. Gerald again told the immigration officers that I was not there, but they barged right past him, and the first place they looked was the balcony. Somehow, and to this very day I do not know how, but I squeezed under a divan bed – the sort of bed that has no legs, just a base with a mattress on top. As the Good Lord would have it, Gerald entered the room first. He saw my foot sticking out from under the bed. Thinking quickly, he grabbed the candle-wick bedspread off the bed and just dropped on my protruding foot. The three immigration officers searched everywhere. They searched the wardrobes; they searched the balcony again. They looked everywhere, and yes, even under the beds. They searched under all the beds in the house, including the one I was under, using flashlights. At one point, one of the officers who was looking under my bed thought he saw something. He ran around the other side of the bed and he shone that flashlight right into my eyes. I closed my eyes, as the light was so bright. I was shaking so hard, I was surprised they did not see the bed shaking. All three officers shone their flashlights under that bed, and to this day I can only believe that God Almighty blinded their eyes so that they just could not see me.

One of the officers told Gerald, 'We know she came in here this morning, because someone saw her come in! We know she is here!' But for the grace of God, I would have been deported out of the country that morning, but that was not God's plan for my life. That was when I truly started knowing the power of God for myself, because I know without a shadow of a doubt, that God showed up in that bedroom that morning and shielded me.

Needless to say, I did not leave the apartment for the rest of the day. I left late that night and moved into my apartment. God had timed everything perfectly! The flat that I found was quite a nice flat. It was at the top of the house in the attic, which had been converted. It was a self-contained flat with its own kitchen and bathroom. It was quite unique in the way it was set up. The bedroom had been elevated. It was built on a sort of platform, so that you had to go up a step to go into the bedroom. Then to go into the living room, which was next to the bedroom, you had to step down. At the other end of the flat was the kitchen, and then I had to go down a couple of steps to the bathroom, which was just outside the door. I loved it.

The owner of the house was of African heritage, and he lived there alone with his daughter, Francis. Francis was beautiful. She was of mixed parentage; her mum was English. Francis was very friendly. She was my age, eighteen, and she was about five foot nine. She had a light complexion and black, curly hair down to the middle of her back. She was of medium build and had hazel eyes. We had a lot in common, except Francis seemed very mature when it came to boys.

She seemed to have a lot of friends who were boys. I, on the other hand, had no friends who were boys.

I was growing up into a beautiful young lady, and I had many admirers, but each time I was asked out by a man, I would simply say, 'I'm sorry. I already have a boyfriend.' This was, of course, untrue, but it did the trick every time. I just did not know how to communicate with boys, so I just avoided them.

Francis and I soon became good friends, and she noticed how awkward I seemed around her friends. When she asked why I did not seem interested in any of her boyfriends, I did not want to tell her about the experience that I had as a child, so I just said I was shy. She then asked me if I was a virgin, to which I responded, 'Don't be silly.' I just pretended that I'd had lots of experience with boys, which, of course, was not true, but I did not want to seem so inexperienced even though, technically, I was a 'relationship virgin', because I had never been in a relationship with a man. Since Mr Nash, I had been too scared to even look at a man let alone have a relationship. Francis seemed happy with my explanation, and I made a point of not being around when her boyfriends came around, so the subject was never raised again.

Now that I was in my own flat, and I was working and going to school at night, I decided that I wanted to send some things to my family back home in Jamaica. I bought a big barrel, and every week, when I got paid, I would buy some items – clothing, soap powder, rice, and all sorts of items for my sisters and brothers and my mother. When the barrel was full, I would ship it out to Jamaica. As soon as I shipped one barrel away, I would replace it with another and repeat the process.

A few months after I moved in, Jane's younger sister, Nadine, invited herself over to my apartment. She was my first guest, and of course I played the perfect hostess. I cooked her a meal, and we watched movies until it was time for her to go home. Nadine, however, like Francis, was curious as to why I was a beautiful girl living alone, and yet I had no friends coming over. She really meant a boyfriend. She opened the subject with, 'So, do you have a boyfriend?' I said, 'Of course I have.' But she knew I was lying, and as she continued to probe, she seemed so excited she could hardly get the questions out quickly enough. It just felt as if she was firing one question after another at me. I needed time to think before I responded. I had to think about what this imaginary boyfriend looked like. What was his name? How tall was he? Where did he live? What was his nationality? How long had we been dating? Did he have a car? Did he have a job? What did he do? Questions, questions, questions!

I guess by my responses and my lack of enthusiasm, she knew that I was lying, so I had to confess there was no boyfriend. The moment I confessed, Nadine made it her duty to get me one. The first thing she did was to turn up at my house the following Saturday night uninvited. She told me we were going out to a club. 'What?' I blurted out. 'A club,' she said. *'No way!'* I said. Nadine then informed me that she was not asking. The subject was not up for debate. I was going. Wow, where had I heard those words before? This bought back a few memories. 'Okay, okay,' I said. 'But I don't have anything to wear!' I thought that would get me off the hook, but no way. Nadine had come prepared. She put make-up on me, and she also did my hair. I had never worn make-up before. She went through my wardrobe and picked out a three-piece pinstripe skirt suit. Those were the days when people really dressed up to go to clubs. Here I was, eighteen years old, and I had never been to a club.

The name of the club was Every Nation. When we got there, I felt very uncomfortable, because having never been to a club before, I did not know what to expect. The club was huge, and was full of people of all different nationalities. I had never seen so many people in one place before. One thing we all seemed to have in common was our age. Almost everyone was young. There were two floors. On the ground floor people were dancing to the latest music, which was fast. Everyone was hot and sweaty, and it was oh so crowded. It seemed to me like the ground floor was for the confident types who wanted to show off their dancing skills. That was not me. The first floor, which is where we went, was a bit more relaxed and less crowded. I was very apprehensive, because I had never danced to this kind of music before. When I was growing up, Elizabeth would say, 'That's the devil's music!' And I was never allowed to sing or dance to the devil's music. Apart from that, I had never danced in public or, even worse, danced with a man.

The girls there seemed so comfortable dancing with different men whilst Nadine and I just danced together. She was a good friend; she danced close by me and never left my side, which I was grateful for. I was way out of my comfort zone. Nadine, on the other hand, was a good dancer and was showing me some of her moves. It did cross my mind that someone might ask me to dance, but I was hoping it wouldn't happen. But then I felt a sharp poke in my side from Nadine. She said, 'Look over there. Do you see those two men?' I turned slightly to look, and to my shock and horror, I realized they were looking straight at us. As I looked, they began making their way over to us.

Nadine started giggling as she said, 'They're going to ask us to dance.' Apparently they had been watching us from the moment we came through the door, but had waited to make sure that we were there alone. One of these two young men was of light complexion, and Nadine was quite dark skinned. I learnt that this young man was named Jonathan. He asked Nadine to dance. The other young man, who was also light skinned, but a bit darker and taller than Jonathan, asked me to dance. I soon learnt his name was Phil.

Phil was five foot eleven, and I thought he was quite handsome. Those were the days when the Afro was in fashion. Phil had a bit of an Afro, which was very well groomed. He was slim and dressed quite nicely. He had on a beautiful, cream-coloured, pure-silk shirt; a pair of black, tailored pants; and black dress shoes, which were highly polished. The first three buttons on his shirt were open – just enough to show off the hair on his chest, and he wore a gold chain around his neck. Phil did not leave my side for the rest of the night, and neither did Jonathan leave Nadine's side. At the end of the night, we exchanged details. Nadine seemed quite taken with Jonathan, but what she didn't know was that all the details I had given to Phil were incorrect. I was so scared, I gave him wrong telephone number and wrong address. Even my name was wrong. I was petrified.

After three months had passed, Jonathan and Nadine were getting on quite well. I was happy for them. One Saturday night I was rather bored, so I decided to go back to the club. It took just about everything I had in me to muster up the courage to go there, especially alone. I figured I had enjoyed it the night I went with Nadine, so why not give it another try? I got all dressed up and made my way there. As I got to the door, I felt a hand grab hold of mine. Lo and behold, it was Phil. He looked me in the eyes and said, 'Ah, now that I have found you, I will never let you go again!' Apparently, he had tried to call me several times, but of course he had discovered the information I had given him was incorrect. He then resorted to standing by the door of the club every Saturday night in the hope that one night I would turn up again.

We spent the whole night together, and this time I gave him my correct details. That Sunday Phil called and asked if he could visit me at home. I said, 'My dad does not allow me to bring boys up to my room.' I made it all up. I needed time to get to know Phil. After what I had been through, I had to be sure. I told Phil that I lived with my dad, and he was very strict, so I could not bring him inside the house. I also told him that Francis was my sister.

It was a year before I would trust Phil enough to tell him that Francis was indeed not my sister, and that her father was my landlord. He seemed angry at first, but then I explained to him that I had been so frightened because of what had happened to me when I was younger. Phil was a gentleman, and he totally understood.

Phil and I got along really well. We did not really argue. We talked a lot, and we were very compatible. His family, on the other hand, were a different story. Phil told me his parents wanted to meet me, and he invited me to dinner at his house. I was very excited and spent some time deciding what to wear, how to comb my hair, what topics might be good for conversation, and that sort of thing. When I got there, his mother, Faye, and his father, Jeremy, were sitting in the dining room. Phil introduced me as his girlfriend, and they both said hello and shook my hand. Faye then beckoned me to take a seat. Faye was about five foot five. She had a fair complexion and a medium built. She wore her black hair short, and she had brown eyes. She did not look the age I presumed her to be, but she reminded me of Elizabeth, my mother, and for all the wrong reasons.

Faye had an angry look on her face, which did not change the whole time I was there. That being said, she was quite an attractive lady. I did not like her demeanour; it scared me and reminded me too much of Elizabeth. There were no smiles, just an angry look. Phil's dad, Jeremy, was approximately five foot ten and had a light complexion. Jeremy wore a cap, and when he removed it, I saw that he was bald from the front to the centre of his head. The rest of his hair, which was black and curly, was cut quite short. He had hazel eyes and was of medium build. I could see the resemblance between Phil and Jeremy. Jeremy was quite a handsome man. He seemed quite pleasant, although he was not very talkative.

Phil's house was huge – five bedrooms on four floors. Inside the front door was a hallway that was quite wide and long. It led onto the first floor, which housed the dining room, which was also used as a family room. Adjoining that was the living room. Both rooms were huge with high ceilings. The decoration was very rich. The carpet was mostly red with other colours. It was more like a Chinese rug in style. A set of stairs led to the three bedrooms on the second floor. On the third floor were two bedrooms – one that Phil's parents shared and another that his two sisters shared. On the fourth floor were another two rooms, one of which Phil's younger brother used. The other room was Phil's, and just off to the right of those two rooms was a small room that no one used. Also from the ground floor, another set of stairs led downstairs into the basement. There was another hallway in the basement. Directly off of this was the kitchen, which was huge. Leading off the kitchen was another huge room, which was used for storage. There was a door that led to the garden. The garden was, again, huge. Jeremy did not seem to be a keen gardener, but he had planted different herbs like thyme and rosemary, and he had planted potatoes. The garden was sectioned off in two parts, one of which accommodated the things Jeremy planted. The other part was just grass. Overall, it was a nice house, but it was badly in need of modernization.

As I sat down after my tour of the house, there was silence. It was an uncomfortable silence. I did not feel very welcome at all. I thought that we were going to sit around the table and talk and eat, and I would get to know Faye and Jeremy, and they would get to know me. I was mistaken. When I got there, Faye and Jeremy had already eaten, and I was just given a plate of food. Phil and I sat together and ate. His two younger sisters, Dreema and Yasmin, and his brother, Simon, would pop in and out of the room, curious as to who I was until Phil introduced me to them.

I really did not feel very comfortable; as a matter of fact, I lost my appetite. But to be polite, of course, I ate. Despite the way Elizabeth had treated me as a child, she had made sure that I knew how to cater for guests, and how to make them feel comfortable. This was definitely not the case here. I found this behaviour a bit strange. How do you invite someone to dinner, and then have your meal without your guest? Phil's dad was very quiet; he did not say much at all. Faye just spent most of the time staring at me, and talking to her son on subjects that centred around me. In effect, she was talking about me whilst I was there, but in an indirect way. I could see that Phil was a bit uncomfortable about this as well. His answers to her questions or comments were very curt. I seriously considered breaking up with Phil at this point, because I wanted a family who would love me for who I was, but I did not feel any love here.

Later, Phil and I had a chat about the situation, and with his charms he managed to convince me that I was not to get upset over this, because that was just the way his parents behaved. I did not quite know what to make of this, but I thought I would give them a chance. After all, I had given Phil a chance! I had not met people who behaved in this manner before in my very sheltered upbringing. I was just not prepared for this. Phil was really not bothered, and he actually told me that his parents liked me. I really did not feel liked at all.

FALLING IN LOVE

As TIME WENT ON, MY relationship with Phil progressed, and I found myself falling in love with him. However, each time we went to his parents' house, I was greeted with the same odd behaviour. Phil was one of six siblings, and he was the middle child. He had an older brother, Jared, who was six foot five with an athletic build, hazel eyes, and a light complexion. He was married and had four children, one girl and three boys. He was followed by a sister, Ruby. Ruby was about five foot five and had brown eyes, a fair complexion, and long hair, which she wore in dreadlocks. Ruby was heavyset and had five children – four girls and a boy. She was followed by Phil, who was followed by another sister, Dreema who was about five foot five and of fair complexion. She had long, shoulder-length, curly, black hair. She was also heavyset. Dreema had a daughter. Dreema was followed by her brother, Simon, who was about five foot seven. He had a dark complexion and short, curly, black hair. Simon was slim and had brown eyes. He had two daughters. Simon was followed by Yasmin, who was about five foot four and of medium build. She had short, black hair; brown eyes; and a very light complexion. She had a daughter.

In the summer of 1979, Phil came to my flat. He was acting strange, but in a good way. We had dinner together, and we were just settling down to watch a movie when, to my surprise, I saw Phil pull a little box from his pocket. My heart stopped – at least it felt as if it had! Right there in the middle of my living room, Phil got down on one knee and asked for my hand in marriage. I was elated, and of course I said yes.

Phil and I had planned to get married as soon as my immigration status had been sorted out, which we hoped would be in the next year or so. This would have taken us to the summer of 1980. I started to get some bridal magazines to give me an idea of the type of things I could do for our wedding. We then began looking at venues, the church, and all the normal things that have to do with planning a wedding. We were both quite excited; that is, until I realized that I had missed my cycle. I thought, *No! This cannot be!* I booked myself an appointment with my doctor, who informed me that I was indeed pregnant. I was not happy, because I wanted to wait until we were married, but it was not to be.

When I told Phil that I was pregnant, he was happy, so that made me happy. The first three months of my pregnancy were horrible. I could not stand the smell of any perfumes, aftershaves, scented soaps, shower gel, deodorant, or even shampoo. I invested in the Simple brand, which was unscented. At the time, it was heaven sent.

For the first three months I did not tell anyone that I was pregnant, not even Phil's parents. I felt so ashamed; I felt that I had let myself down. I was a small person, and I carried really small, so no one even noticed my growing stomach. At three months, Phil told his parents that we were expecting, and they did not seem too bothered, so I just got on with being pregnant. His sisters, on the other hand, seemed quite excited about the baby, as it was our first child. The rest of the pregnancy was uneventful. I was barely showing at seven months.

A few days later, I went to the antenatal clinic for my regular check up, and the doctor told me that the baby's head was engaged. I had no idea what this meant, and he did not seem bothered about it, so I did not let it bother me either. I was soon to find out exactly what that meant! I had gone to the clinic on the Thursday, and on the Sunday morning, I was relaxing in bed at my girlfriend Nadine's house. Nadine had popped out to the shop, and when she got back she rang the doorbell. I got up out of bed to open the door for her, and as I did so, I felt a great whoosh of water coming from my body. I looked down and saw a puddle on the floor. I had no idea what to do.

Nadine asked me if I was in any pain. I said no, because I felt just fine. If this was how childbirth was, I could do this, no pain! I was only seven months pregnant. Nadine called my doctor, who told her that I needed to go to the hospital immediately. He explained that, although I was in no pain, the baby was no longer protected in the amniotic sac. My water had broken, which left the baby susceptible to infections.

Nadine dialled 999, and the ambulance came. The paramedics were very attentive and kept asking me all the way to the hospital if I was in any pain. I was getting a little irritated with being asked constantly, 'Are you in any pain?' *What's this pain everyone keeps asking me about? Do they not realize I am going to make history and have an early, pain-free delivery?* Oh, how I wished this would be true. Little did I know what was to come!

When I got to the hospital, I was admitted. The doctors told me that they did not want me to go into labour, as it was too soon to deliver the baby. They gave me an injection to delay labour and ordered that I be hooked up to a monitor that would monitor the baby's heartbeat. This would tell them when and if I was having contractions. I was only twenty-eight weeks pregnant. I started getting some pain on Tuesday, but because this was my first child, I just told myself that I was experiencing a lot of gas, and that was what was causing the pain. I failed to mention the pain to the nurses or the doctor. Although I was hooked up to a monitor that was registering the pain, because I did not tell them I was in pain, they failed to take any notice of the monitor readings.

Phil came in to see me, and I was telling him that the gas pain seemed to be getting worse and worse. The lady in the bed next to me had been watching me, and overheard me telling Phil about the gas pain. By this time, it was Thursday afternoon; I had been experiencing the pain for two days. When she heard me describe the pains, she started laughing and said, 'That's not gas, love! You're in labour!'

I rang the buzzer to let the nurse know I was in pain, and she came over and looked at the monitor. I saw sheer panic on her face. I was indeed in labour, and I was fully dilated and ready to deliver. The nurse wheeled me straight to the delivery room, and I delivered a healthy three-pound-fourteen-ounce baby boy at twenty-eight weeks. Phil and I named him Phil Junior. He was taken away from me immediately. I did not see him when I delivered him, but Phil did. He went with Phil Junior to the premature baby's unit, and the midwife and doctors attended to me. I asked to see my baby, but I was not able to see him until the next day, as I was completely out of it that evening having received pain medication, which seemed to have knocked me out.

Childbirth was not at all how I expected it to be; it was far worse. I was in so much pain. However, the next day, I was taken in a wheelchair to see my baby for the first time. He was just a little bit bigger than a bag of sugar. The nurses had to put a pillow in my lap, and they showed me how to lay him on the pillow and hold him safely. He was just so fragile, so tiny, but so perfect. I was so in love with my son. I now realized why Phil had been so excited and happy the night before. He had been the happiest I had ever seen him. He was now a father for the first time, and I was now a mother! Me – a mother at twenty-one years old!

Our baby was so tiny. He had a mop of straight, black hair. His little hands and feet were so perfect. He was so white; it was difficult to tell that he was not of white parents. I loved this little boy. He was the most beautiful baby in the whole wide world. On the day I gazed into the face of my beautiful son, I made up this declaration: 'Whenever you see a pregnant woman, always assume that there is beauty there'! I was just blown away. The nurses later told me that, whenever I was holding my son, they would speak to me, but I would just ignore them. In truth, I was in my own little world with my son. It was a world in which, at that time, no one else existed – just the two of us.

Phil was just like a cat that got the cream; he was just beside himself. He loved his son. The next day, the family started coming around to see the baby, and everyone seemed to love him. Phil's parents had a tradition in their family. Faye and Jeremy would not go to the hospital to see any of the babies born into the family. They would wait until the babies were discharged from the hospital before they would see them. Phil Junior, however, would be the exception to that rule. We were told that Phil Junior was going to be in the hospital for a while, so Phil's mother decided to come and see him there.

Phil was just so excited that his mother was coming to see his son, his first child. I was wheeled to the premature unit again. This is where I spent most of my days with my baby. I was there when Phil's mother came to see Phil Junior. I was devastated when I heard her say, 'But this *ya citen* can't live!' (This thing cannot live!) I have never forgotten those words, and I could not believe that anyone could be that insensitive. I wished she had not bothered to come to the hospital. She referred to my child as a thing, not even a person.

A week and a half later, I was discharged from the hospital, but Phil Junior had to stay there until he had reached a weight of five pounds, at which time he could be discharged. I would visit Phil Junior at the hospital every day; indeed, I spent most of my days with him, expressing my milk so that he could be fed through the tube that was attached to his face. It was heartbreaking seeing the tube on his face, because he was so hairy. Every time the nurses changed the tube, it was as if they were taking a piece of me away.

The day finally came, however, a month later, when Phil Junior could be discharged from the hospital. He now weighed exactly five pounds. Phil and I were so happy to be taking our baby home. He was still so tiny that even the newborn-size clothes were too big for him. These days they have premature sizes, but back then they were non-existent.

Our first stop on the way home from the hospital was to Phil's parents' home. As I mentioned earlier, Phil's parents would not go to the hospital to visit the newborn babies in the family, so it was customary that, before the new baby would go home, the parents would go to Phil's parents' home to show off the new baby. Although Faye had made an exception and had come to the hospital, Phil's dad, Jeremy, had not yet seen his newest grandson, so that is why we stopped at their house. Phil's dad did not say much, but you could tell from his smiles that he was happy to meet little Phil Junior.

After a few hours, I was exhausted, and Phil and I decided to head on home with Phil Junior. Phil Junior was such a contented baby. He slept pretty much most of the night that first night, and it did not take him long to sleep through the night. Phil grew and grew, and he got so fat I could hardly carry him with my small frame. I was told at the baby clinic that premature babies developed very fast, and Phil was proof of this. When he was a few months old, no one could tell that he had come into the world weighing just three pounds, fourteen ounces.

By this time, I had finished my studies, and I was working as a personal assistant for the director in a bank. I loved my job. Although I could have taken more time off to be at home, I was excited to go back to work. Being a stay-at-home mother was *not* for me. I loved my baby, but I hated the being-at-home part, so when Phil Junior was three months old, I left him with his grandmother (Phil's mom), who was a registered childminder, and I went back to work. I loved coming home to my baby; he was gorgeous.

THE ULTIMATE BETRAYAL

PHIL JUNIOR WAS THREE MONTHS old, and Phil and I had not had even one night out. Phil suggested that we go back to the club where we first met. I was excited ! I had my hair done, and I got a beautiful black dress. Of course, I had no baby weight; I was actually smaller than I had been when I fell pregnant. I felt and looked beautiful. When we went to the club, Every Nation, Phil and I danced the night away. I was having a wonderful time. At about three in the morning we were both feeling very tired, so we decided to take a break from dancing. We went upstairs to sit in one of the lounges. They were like little private rooms. Now I was a very confident woman when it came to my man, because I was a beautiful woman, although it had taken me some time to realize this. I had a great figure, and I had hair down to the middle of my back – and this was not a weave; this was my own hair. After my difficult past, I had worked for many years to build up this confidence and believe in myself. I knew Phil was an attractive man, so I was used to women throwing themselves at him, but I figured he had eyes only for me.

Oh, what a hard lesson to learn. Never swear for your man. Never say never! This life has a way of proving you wrong. As I was sitting there in the club, I saw a young woman approach our room. I noticed that Phil sprang to his feet rather swiftly. Then he went outside the room to talk to her. Still, I was not bothered, because, as I said, I was a confident woman. Phil worked in the clothing industry, and his job required him to speak to a lot of women on a daily basis. I was certainly not the jealous type. However, this young woman got my attention when I heard her yell at Phil, 'Gimme back my keys!' I had been resting my head on the table, but I soon lifted it up when I heard those words. Strangely, I was no longer tired. I watched carefully as I saw Phil take a key from his key ring and hand it to her. I heard Phil tell her that I was his wife, and we had just had a baby. This woman walked off, and she seemed very angry.

Phil came back into the room, and I noticed he would not maintain eye contact with me. *Strange*, I thought. Throughout the night he had done nothing but gaze into my eyes. His encounter with the woman had left a bitter taste in my mouth, so I told Phil I wanted to go home. I waited until we got into our car, and I then I started to question Phil as to why he'd had this young lady's key. He tried his best to fob me off, but I was having none of it, because I had heard quite clearly what she had said to Phil. I think he was hoping that I hadn't heard her.

Phil decided to come clean and tell me everything. I was devastated. Whilst I was pregnant with our first son, Phil was out there having an affair. I felt as if my whole world had collapsed. I did not know what to do. One part of me wanted nothing more to do with Phil, but when I looked at little Phil Junior, our little boy, I didn't know if it would be right for me to deny him of having his dad around. I certainly knew what it was like growing up without a father, and I did not want my son to suffer as I had. It was so hard. I could not even look at Phil. I could not bear for him to touch me. I was heartbroken.

Phil could not apologize enough. He would have done anything to make our relationship work, and I figured everyone messes up at some time, so I decided to give him another chance. He promised me that the relationship had been a one off, and it would never happen again. He seemed so sincere, and I believed him.

No sooner had I decided to give Phil another chance, that he came home and told me he had gotten a disease from that girl, and I needed to go and get checked out. I told him there was no way I was going to that clinic alone – he was coming with me. He quickly agreed. He took me to the clinic. I had never been so humiliated in my entire life. I had to put my legs in stirrups, and the doctor attended to me. I had contracted gonorrhea from Phil. I felt at this time that I could literally kill Phil with my bare hands, I was that angry.

It took some time before I could even begin to trust Phil again. I had made the decision to stay with him for the sake of our child, so I had to make peace with the situation within myself. I simply had to learn to trust Phil all over again, because without trust, you cannot have a meaningful relationship. I told Phil when he asked me to marry him that I would do so on two conditions. First, he would never lay his hands on me. Second, he would never cheat on me! I told him everything else I could work with. I had told him that, if ever he did either of these two things, we would be finished. Here I was being tested at a time when I was at my most vulnerable. I had just given birth!

THE ARRIVAL OF ELIZABETH

I T WAS AROUND THIS TIME that my mother, Elizabeth, started asking me if she could come over from Jamaica to see me. I wanted to see her, because by now it had been over four years since I had seen her. I did not feel that this was the right time for her to come, however, because Phil Junior was only six months old, and Phil and I had only a one-bedroom flat. Where would we put her to sleep? We were a young couple just starting out in life, and had no help apart from working ourselves.

Our flat was sparsely furnished. It was a nice, sixth-floor flat in an affluent area. The bedroom was quite big. It fitted our queen-sized bed with two bedside tables, each with a lamp; Phil Junior's crib; and our wardrobe. The floor was not carpeted; it was wooden floor, but we had bought a big rug, which gave the room a warm, homely feeling.

The living room consisted of a three-seater sofa and two single chairs. These were used, and not gently used. They were really used. They had been given to me by a friend of the family, and we were grateful for them. Being the optimistic person that I am, I had gone out and bought covers for the sofa and chairs, which made them look a bit more presentable. We had a coffee table, a few plants, and also a TV. All were used items. In the kitchen we had a stove and cooking utensils – not much of anything, but enough to get us by.

So you see, it was not that I did not want my mother to come over; I just didn't know how we was going to accommodate her. Elizabeth did not see my point of view and became upset. She thought I did not want her around me, but that could not have been further from the truth. Despite her treatment of me as a child, I loved my mother, but she just did not understand. I ended up telling Elizabeth to go ahead and come over, because I did not want us to fall out with each other.

So after a month of corresponding back and forth, Elizabeth came to England. It's amazing how the tables had turned. When I was a child growing up, Elizabeth treated me so badly, calling me some terrible names and telling me just how nasty I was. As you can imagine, it was such a shock to me when Elizabeth came to stay with me that she was so untidy. Yes, that is the word I will choose to use. Whenever she would cook in the kitchen, she would light the stove and then just throw the used matches on the floor. I found myself constantly picking up and cleaning up after her. I guess I had not noticed her habits when I was a child, because it was my job to do those things for her, but now as an adult, I clearly saw that I was not the one who was untidy; it was Elizabeth.

I told my brother, James, that his mom was visiting. As you will recall, James had been sent to England when he was ten years old to live with his dad. He seemed quite excited at the news of her upcoming visit. At this point, James had not seen Elizabeth for thirteen years. He was now twenty-three. He came over to see Elizabeth all excited, but he was there for probably only fifteen minutes before he left abruptly. He literally ran out of the house. I called after him, but he did not respond. A few days later, I managed to speak to James, and he told me that the reason he had left so abruptly was that he did not think Elizabeth was his mom. I tried to persuade him to come back and to talk with her, and he would find out that she was indeed his mom. Although Elizabeth was with me for six months, James never came back to see her. Did he know something I didn't?

Elizabeth had cousins in America, and all of a sudden she decided that she wanted to go to see them, this is despite the fact that she had come over to England with no money. I guess when I was telling Elizabeth before she came over that I did not have the money or the space to accommodate her, she did not believe me. Now she was witnessing first hand my struggles. I told Phil that Elizabeth wanted to go to America, and he said, 'Okay, if that's what she wants to do, then we will help her to get there.' Phil and I got our pennies together. We saved up and booked Elizabeth's flight, paying her fare, and we gave her some money. She went to America to her cousins, who were Gerald's sisters. Again, Elizabeth had never met them. I discovered that, whilst I was at work, Elizabeth would be on the phone with these people, which of course left me with a huge telephone bill.

I was getting stressed with Elizabeth being with us, because she was not helping me, but she did not seem to care about that. As long as Elizabeth got what she wanted, that was all that mattered. This was to become even more evident in the months to come. I wore prescription glasses. The day after Elizabeth had left, I discovered that I could not find my glasses. I searched just about everywhere I could think of, but just could not find them. They had been very expensive, as I had chosen to have designer frames. Out of desperation, I called Elizabeth in America to ask her if she had seen my glasses, to which she responded that she had not seen them. I resigned myself to the fact that I would just have to get new ones, and as they were not cheap, I would have to save up again for them. I felt quite annoyed with myself. How could I be this careless with my glasses?

A year went by, and I had just managed to buy another pair of glasses. Gerald's sister, Jean – the one who had met me at the airport – went to America to visit her sisters. When she came to visit me upon her return, she just happened to mention that she had seen Elizabeth wearing some glasses. She said that Elizabeth could not even see to walk when she was wearing them; she would step high, because she could not see where she was going properly. I asked Jean to describe the glasses, and sure enough, they were mine. I was devastated. At no time had it even crossed my mind that my own mother would steal from me. What mother would steal her daughter's glasses, especially prescription glasses? They were no good to Elizabeth, but she had taken them anyway. That was the thanks I got for Phil and I saving up, and not only paying her fare to go to America, but also giving her money to spend when she got there.

A few days later, my devastation turned to anger, and I felt that I needed to hear Elizabeth herself tell me that she had taken my glasses. I was still in denial. I could not believe that she would do such a thing, so I called her on the telephone and asked her outright, 'Did you take my glasses?' Her response was, 'Yes I did! And so what? You can buy another one!' Wow, wow, wow! That just said it all for me. There was no apology, just rudeness. But, what did I expect? I decided that I needed some time away from Elizabeth, so I made a conscious decision that I would not speak to her for a while. I needed to calm down, because I did not want to say something to my mother that would displease God. The Bible says, 'Honor your father and your mother, so that you may live long in the land the Lord your God is giving you' (Exodus 20:12 New International Version). I was not about to dishonour my mother. No way! It was not unusual for me to not speak to Elizabeth for prolonged periods of time, because during the time when I was living with Gerald and his family, I would speak to her only once, maybe twice a year if I was lucky. Not surprisingly, Elizabeth made no attempt to contact me except when she wanted money.

When Phil Junior was born, he looked like his dad, but as he grew, he started to look just like me. He was a beautiful baby with his mop of curly, black hair. Phil's younger sister, Yasmin, absolutely adored him. Phil Junior's hair was so long, Yasmin would cornrow it every opportunity she got. He was so chunky, and his cheeks were targets for everyone to kiss. He was adorable. It wasn't long before we were celebrating Phil's first birthday. We threw him a big party. I don't know if the kids who came to his party had fun, but I know I sure did! Let's face it, a one-year-old has no idea what's going on. I say we gave the child a party, but if I'm really honest, I have to say that the party was more for the grown-ups. Most of the children who came were Phil's age or older, and of course all his cousins were there and the parents of his cousins, so it was pretty much a family affair as well. In these cases you have two parties, one for the children and one for the grown-ups, which means you need to cater for the grown-ups too. We had all the normal children's food – cake, jelly, and ice cream, along with finger foods such as chicken nuggets, drumsticks, sandwiches, and so forth. For the grown-ups, we had curry goat and rice with salad, coleslaw, and some barbecue ribs. We also had fried snapper. It was a lot of work, but well worth it. The party went really well. All our guests expressed their gratitude for the invitation, and also stated what a great time they had. Phil and I enjoyed our first birthday party for our son.

PREGNANT AGAIN

EXACTLY EIGHT MONTHS LATER, I discovered I was pregnant again. This time there was no mistaking the symptoms. I was very nauseous the first three months. I was still not able to tolerate the smell of anything scented such as deodorant, perfumes, and so forth. Again the Simple range of products was heaven sent. Phil and I decided that we would not tell anyone until I was three months pregnant. So around the three-month mark, we told his parents. They were very nonchalant. They pretty much would not comment or ask any questions. The rest of his family were pretty happy, especially Phil's youngest sister, Yasmin. Yasmin made quite a fuss of me whenever I was around.

Time seemed to go so fast this time around. I carried on working right up to the last minute. The idea was that I would be able to spend more time with the baby when he or she was born. In those days, there was no routine test to determine the sex of the baby; you just had to wait until the baby was born to find out.

One night, whilst Phil and I were in bed at around three in the morning, I rolled over to my side and, as I did so, I felt a trickle of water. I thought this was odd, and rolled over unto my other side. Again I felt a trickle of water. Not wanting to wake Phil, I got up and walked to the bathroom to check out what was happening. I was none the wiser. I just felt a little uncomfortable, which I simply attributed to being heavily pregnant. I did not feel ready to go back to bed, so I went to sit in the living room for a moment. As I did so, I felt a whoosh. I looked on the floor and could see and feel the water.

Again, just as before, my water had broken. I was just barely eight months pregnant. Only this time it was different – I was actually in pain. I woke Phil to tell him that we needed to go to the hospital. Now.

Phil just did not seem to be coping, partly, I think, because he was still half asleep, and partly because he was scared. What did he have to be scared about? Shouldn't I be the one to be scared? I say this because Phil had put his jumper inside out, and he was dressing our son in his jumper, also inside out. As we are told to do at antenatal classes, I was very prepared for such an occurrence so, of course, my bag was packed. After what had happened the last time, I didn't want to be taking any chances.

Phil was running out of the house when I called him, and I said, 'Honey, my bag.' He asked, 'What bag?' I said, 'My bag that I need to take to the hospital.' Phil said, 'Oh, okay.' Again he was going through the door without my bag. I said, 'Phil!' He turned and looked at me and he said, 'Your bag. Right.' I said, 'Right.' And we both started laughing.

We had arranged with Phil's sister, Ruby, that she would keep Phil Junior whenever I went into labour. Ruby lived a short distance away from us, so on our way to the hospital, we dropped Phil Junior off. I was in a lot of pain, and Phil was driving quite fast on the way to the hospital. I think he thought I was going to have that baby right there and then. He was just not prepared for that, so his reaction was to put his foot down. Of course, this was not good, because we were pulled over by the police. Phil explained the situation to the officer. As soon as the officer looked into the car and got a look at me, he escorted us to the hospital. This was good, as it got us there a whole lot faster.

When I got to the hospital, the midwife examined me; I was already eight centimetres dilated. This labour was progressing very fast. From not feeling any pain to being eight centimetres in the space of an hour was incredible. I think I must have been in labour whilst at home in bed, but slept through most of it. By this time, the pain was really kicking in, I was in agony, and I was begging for some pain relief. Of course, because I was so far along, I could have only gas and air (nitrous oxide and oxygen, also known as laughing gas). I really wanted the good stuff like the epidural, which would allow me to just relax and feel no pain, but that was not to be.

Within two hours, Timothy came into the world, a healthy baby boy weighing five pounds exactly. This weight was fantastic, because unlike his brother, Phil Junior, Timothy did not need to spend any extra time in the hospital. Although he was small, he was totally fine. He was a gorgeous little boy; like his brother, he had a mop of straight, black hair with a curl at the front of his head. To this day, he still has that curl. He was so white – again just like his brother. It was difficult to tell he was not Caucasian. He was just so perfect. What struck me the most about Timothy was that he was the image of his dad, Phil. Timothy did not look at all like me. He had Phil's eyes, his nose, his mouth. Just about everything of Timothy was Phil's. He was like a clone of Phil. I felt as if I was just a vessel that had bought Timothy into this world. He was just all Phil.

When Timothy was born and I held him for the first time, he just lay in my arms, content to just look around the room with his knuckles in his mouth, eating his fingers. It has been said that new-born babies are not able to see. I beg to differ. Timothy was following movements around the room; he could certainly see. He was, right from the beginning, such a contented little baby. I just loved my little bundle of joy. I did not want to put him down.

That evening the family came around, and of course everyone commented about just how much Timothy looked like his dad. The highlight of the evening was, of course, introducing Phil Junior to his baby brother. Phil brought Phil Junior to the hospital. Once he had settled in, we sat Phil Junior on the bed and put little Timothy in his arms. Phil Junior, who was just two years old at the time, sat there for a minute or so just looking at his brother. All of a sudden, and without warning, he gave a great big push. Phil Junior decided that he no longer wanted to hold his brother. It's good that the boys' dad had good reflexes, because if he hadn't, Timothy would have been on the floor! We knew then that we would have to watch Phil Junior with Timothy. I believe Phil Junior was none too happy. He had been an only child up to now. All of a sudden this other little person had come along and was taking the attention away from him, and he was not happy.

Timothy and I were doing just fine. I had been in hospital for four days, and most of the family had been in to see us, and also friends. I was getting ready to be discharged, but I did not feel well all throughout the day. When the nursing staff changed over that evening, the nurse took one look at me and said, 'You don't look too good.' I told her I didn't feel too good. She took my temperature and realized I had a high fever. I had picked up an infection in the hospital called streptococcus. This was a problem, as I was allergic to penicillin, the antibiotic that would have been the most effective to treat this infection. The infection had entered my blood stream and was proving quite difficult to treat without the penicillin. I was quite ill for forty-eight hours and had to be fed through a tube. I had drips everywhere. When I finally recovered, the nurse told me that they thought they were going to lose me that first night. This was echoed by the patients on either side of my bed. I had to spend an extra week in the hospital.

Finally it was time to go home, and of course, as customary in Phil's family, we had to make a stop at his parents' home for them to welcome the new baby into the family. When we got there, Faye and Jeremy awaited us eagerly, as the rest of the family had expressed just how much Timothy looked like his dad. When they saw Timothy, both Faye and Jeremy were stunned. They were so taken aback at just how much Timothy looked like his dad. Of course they just loved him straight away. I didn't know if this was good or bad, but only time would tell.

TIME TO BUY A HOUSE

W̲E HAD MOVED INTO A brand-new, two-bedroom flat, and
it was only two floors high. It was in a nice area, and I
loved it. It was so modern, and we had settled in just in
time to welcome little Timothy home. Phil and I started discussions
about buying a house, because we wanted our children to have their
own garden to play in, and we wanted them to feel safe when playing. If we had a house of our own, with a garden, then our children
wouldn't have to play in the street.

Phil and I started looking around for a house. We decided that
it would make sound sense to move closer to his family, as the children would be going to his mother whilst Phil and I were both at
work. These were difficult times. Because we really wanted to move
to the other side of London, we had to take quite a journey every
time we had to view a property. It would take us at least an hour and
a half to drive to see the property, and we would usually have the
children with us. Of course, it would take us the same amount of
time to get back home.

After several wasted journeys, Phil and I decided to combine
our viewings so we could go out only once per week, and we would
look at properties in a selected area instead of driving from one part of
the city to another. Phil wanted a property with a garage and enough
space to park his van, which he used for work. I, on the other hand,
wanted a place that had a big kitchen. We started arguing almost every
time we viewed a property. Somehow the properties we were viewing
just didn't seem to have both. Either the property would have a nice
big kitchen, but there would be nowhere for Phil to park his van. Or,
it would have a nice garage and plenty of parking space, but a dingy
little kitchen. There just didn't seem to be any compromise.

After months of looking at properties, Phil and I were getting quite fed up. We were actually thinking of taking a break for a while. We decided to look at one last property. When we pulled up to this property, we had just viewed a different property, and we were in the middle of a blazing row. However, when we looked up at this last property, we both stopped dead in our tracks. We could not believe this was the property. We quickly checked the address, and it seemed correct. The agent, however, was not there, so we were quite suspicious, because for the money they were asking, no way could this be the property. It just seemed too good to be true.

Phil quickly called the agent, who informed us he was on his way. Whilst waiting for the agent, we decided to look around the outside of the property. We peeked into the garden; the grass was about six feet high. We knew we would have our work cut out for us. There was a garage and a driveway in front of the garage that would accommodate Phil's van and a car. At the front of the house there was additional parking space for another car. This was great, just what we were looking for.

Nothing, however, could have prepared us for the inside of the property. Just like the outside, the inside really needed attention. The wallpaper was orange with tiny printed flowers, and the curtains were bright orange. The carpet was also bright orange. It was as if we were trapped in the past. There was no central heating, only small electric heaters on the walls, one in each bedroom and in the bathroom. The kitchen was so dingy, but there was a lot of space to expand.

This was a three-bedroom house, and for the first time both Phil and I were excited about a property. We were at last in agreement, especially when Phil and I made a deal. He promised me that he would have a kitchen built to my specification, and I agreed. I was *happy*! The back garden was huge. There was so much potential in this property, we decided to go ahead and make the purchase. It was exciting, because it was as if we were starting from scratch. I would totally get to redecorate the whole house. Phil, I thought, would enjoy getting the garden into some sort of shape, and I would totally enjoy putting my stamp on this place that we were about to call home.

Moving into Our New House

THINGS MOVED ALONG QUITE NICELY, and we moved into the house on 3 November 1982. I wish I could say it was bliss, but it was far from bliss. We certainly had a lot of work to do. That winter was particularly brutal in terms of the cold, and it was probably one of the hardest decisions we had to make to make the move in the dead of winter. The flat we were moving out of, as I previously mentioned, was brand new, so it was nice and warm. Moving into this house was a huge test. We put the two boys to sleep in one room in one bed, and we put about three duvets on them to be sure they would be warm. Phil and I would take turns in the mornings getting out of bed to turn on the electric heaters. We would each try to cheat by saying, 'I did it yesterday, so it's your turn!' So we would turn on our heater in our bedroom, then we would turn on the heater in the boys' room, and then we would turn on the heater in the bathroom. This did not go on for very long. Within a month, Phil got workers in to install central heating. Oh! The first day that the heating was on we all felt as if we were in heaven.

The second thing we did in the house was remodel the bathroom. It was so old. We ripped out all the fixtures and put in a nice new bathroom set. The wall tiles were like something from Noah's ark, so we installed new ones. After that we turned our attention to rewiring the electric system. The wires and plugs that were there were ancient. This was getting expensive. Every penny Phil and I had would go to buy something for the house.

Disaster struck! Our elder son, Phil Junior, got up early one morning when his dad got up to go to work. He just wanted to spend some time with his dad. Phil Junior went downstairs into the storage cupboard in the kitchen to get a toilet roll. Phil was in the bathroom, and I was still in bed. It was 5.30 in the morning. Phil had got up and had gone through his usual routine, which included boiling the kettle to make himself a cup of tea. Because the wiring in the house needed to be redone, in order to boil the kettle, we had to use an extension plug, which ran across the kitchen floor. Neither Phil nor I realized that Phil Junior had gone downstairs. Usually this would not have been an issue, because the children were usually in bed until after we were up, and we would have removed the cord by then.

However, as Phil Junior decided to get up on this fateful day, and go downstairs without our knowledge, he tripped on the wire. The kettle had just boiled. We were alerted to the disaster by his screams, and I jumped out of the bed and followed Phil, who had already made his way downstairs. The boiling water had gone over the back of Phil Junior's leg. I could see the bubbles starting to form. I was devastated. I started crying; I couldn't take seeing his pain. We quickly got Timothy dressed and took Phil Junior to the hospital. The doctors and nurses attended to him, but they started asking us questions about how he had got burnt. They seemed quite suspicious of Phil and me. At this point I was about to lose my temper, but Phil explained to me that they were only doing their jobs. They had to inform Social Services in order to protect children and stop child abuse.

Phil Junior's vocabulary was fantastic, and he was able to tell the nurses what had happened. They were having trouble understanding how he got burnt on the back of his leg. When we explained how this had happened, the nurses then asked Phil Junior separately in another room, and they were finally satisfied that it was just an accident. I couldn't quite fathom that people would actually cause such harm to their children on purpose. I was upset just thinking that they thought I was capable of doing that to my baby.

PLANNING OUR WEDDING

I T WAS NOW LATE 1983, two years since we bought our house, and it was also time for Phil and I to get married. The moment Phil and I decided we were going to have a wedding, I called Elizabeth and told her of our plans. I said that, of course, we wanted her there. After all, she was my mother. To my surprise, Elizabeth's reaction was, 'I don't have any money to come over there.' I was surprised, as I knew that she was working, and I was her first child to get married. She would have plenty of time to save up; I was telling her two years in advance!

We had been working on the wedding plans for the past year. The church was now booked; the hall was booked. I had chosen my bridesmaids and my flower girls. I decided that Phil's eldest sister, Ruby, would be my maid of honour, and his two younger sisters would my bridesmaids, along with my three cousins. My two nieces would be my flower girls. There would be eight bridal attendants in total.

I had also chosen my dress; it was from a very popular bridal shop. Before we decided to get married, whenever I passed that shop, I always saw the most stunning dresses in the window. It was no surprise, then, that this was the first shop that I looked in. The dresses were divine, and I was very petite, so I chose a stunning off-the-shoulder number in ivory. It was absolutely gorgeous. I was in love with this dress. I had decided that I would not buy my dress; I would hire it. The assistant had me try on the dress, and she would make the necessary alterations. I was to go back two weeks before my wedding day to try the dress one last time before the big day.

Phil had chosen his best man and his groomsmen, and we had got together to choose their outfits as well. We had chosen the caterers and the photographer. It was now time to start looking at wedding invitations and also to select someone who would be able to make the programs for the church service. We had also chosen the cake and the florist. Generally, we were getting everything in order for the big day.

In those days, alcohol was a must at any wedding, and this was usually the largest expense apart from the catering. I came up with a plan that I thought would enable Phil and I to have enough alcohol at our wedding without having to do the 'big spend' at the actual time of the wedding, when we would probably be low on funds. I decided that, in order to make things easier, every week when I did our weekly grocery shopping, I would pick up a bottle of liquor – gin, brandy, rum, and so forth. My plan worked really well, because after a year I had accumulated at least fifty-two bottles of liquor. Some weeks I would even double up if any particular drink was on sale.

Three months before the wedding it was time to send out our invitations. Despite the fact that Elizabeth had said she would not be attending, I still sent her an invitation. I thought that this might prompt her to reconsider. I was her first daughter, and I was getting married. Why was my mother not even excited for me? All throughout the planning stage, Elizabeth had not once called me to offer any form of support, encouragement, or even help. Oh, I could have done with the help of my mother, but I guess I was learning that, in that department, I was on my own. That hurt so much. I looked at other girls getting married, and their moms were there to help them, to give them a hug, to say, 'Don't worry. Everything is going to be all right.' Where was Elizabeth? Planning a wedding is very stressful, and it is hard work, especially if you are on foot.

At the time I had not yet passed my driving test, and I knew I needed to accomplish that, so amidst all the chaos that was taking place with wedding planning, I decided to add driving lessons to the agenda. This was made even more difficult, as I decided to have my lessons in secret. I hated failure, and I knew if I mentioned I wanted to take lessons, Phil would offer to pay for them, bit I wanted that bit of independence. I figured I would not need to spend money on a car, because Phil used a van for work, and every day our car was just parked in the driveway; we used it only on the weekends. I continued my secret lessons, and the time came when I needed to take my test. I knew Phil would be at work and the boys would be at their grandma's, so I would have the time to relax my mind. It didn't quite work that way. On the day of the test, I was so stressed out. My instructor gave me some tablets called Kalms, which were specifically designed for situations such as this. After taking these two little pills, I felt much more relaxed. I took my driving test. When it was over, the examiner said, 'I am pleased to inform you that you have passed.' My reaction wasn't at all what I expected – I just burst out crying! But these were tears of joy, because this was my third test, and finally I heard those magic words.

When I got back to my driving instructor's car, I was still crying. He thought that I had failed my test until he saw me holding the piece of paper in my hand. By this time I was head over heels in wedding preparation. Passing my test could not have come at a better time. I needed to do a lot of last-minute things for the wedding, and being able to drive was just the icing on the cake. It just made my life so much easier.

I had planned just how I would tell Phil that I had passed my test; here's how I did it. I went to the shop and bought the biggest bottle of champagne that they had, and I started celebrating all by myself. Then I called Phil and I said to him, 'Guess what I did today?' Curiously he said, 'What did you do?' And I told him I'd just passed my driving test. He was shocked. He had not known I was even taking lessons. It just felt so good.

The very next day, I was driving our car, a Toyota Celica. I loved that car. It was now just two weeks before our wedding. Time to go back and try my dress again. Oh, I was so excited, but not for long! I got to the shop with my maid of honour, Ruby, and when the assistant bought out the dress that I had chosen, I was very disappointed. When I had tried the dress on previously, it was new. However, this dress must have been very popular, because it just seemed so tatty, as it had been hired out so many times. I was very upset, and told the assistant that I would not be getting married in that dress because of the condition it was in. I left the shop in tears. It was two weeks before my wedding day, and I did not have a dress!

Ruby and I decided to go to another wedding shop, which was not too far away, and I decided to purchase a dress instead. I tried on a few dresses, and I then settled on a beautiful white lace dress. It was full of character. It was not at all like the other dress. The other dress was more of a fun dress, but this dress was a real dress-up kind of dress. It was very Victorian. It had puffed sleeves, and it was an A-line cut, which really looked nice on me. The neck was high, which somehow emphasized my bust line, and there was a beautiful rose on the side in the front of the dress. It even had a long train. I loved it, and I decided to buy it. There was a beautiful veil that really complimented the dress, so I got that as well.

Right after I purchased the new dress, a representative from the company with which I had arranged to hire the original dress called me. She was very apologetic and told me they did not want to cause me stress so close to my wedding. She informed me that they had just received some brand-new dresses from Paris, and although they were more expensive, they would allow me to hire any one I wanted at the same price I was going to pay for the first one. Alas, it was all too late. I'd already purchased my dress. I informed them of this decision, and they gave me a full refund.

The closer we got to our wedding day, the faster the days seemed to be moving along. We were now only a week away from our wedding day. I found myself bursting out crying all of a sudden at different times; in fact, I cried every day right up until the day before our wedding.

A week before our wedding, my bridesmaids decided to throw me a hen party. They took me to a wine bar, and they tried to get me as drunk as they possibly could. It was a good night; fun was had by all. In the meantime, Phil's groomsmen decided to throw him a stag do. He was very tight lipped about the whole affair, but one thing I got from him was that he had fun, and that was all that mattered.

I planned to stay at Phil's parent's house on the eve of our wedding, because that was where all the bridesmaids would be getting dressed. It made perfect sense that I should be there as well, in view of the fact also that we were all going to the hairdresser first thing on my wedding day. Somehow, there was such a sadness in my heart and a yearning, because I was hoping deep down that Elizabeth would surprise me and show up for my big day. I wanted my mom so badly. I decided to stay home all alone, because I thought that Elizabeth would at least call me to wish me well on my wedding day. It was also a time for me to reflect and be calm and get out anything that was on my mind and be totally prepared for my big day. I listened out for the phone all night long, as there is a five-hour difference in time between England and America.

MY WEDDING DAY

I HAD TO LEAVE THE HOUSE at 7.30 on the morning of my wedding to get to the hairdresser, and right up to that time Elizabeth had not called me! I got up so early that morning. I was excited and nervous all at the same time. I could not believe that the day was here at last. Our car had been washed the day before, but there I was on my wedding day at six in the morning washing the car. I needed something to keep me occupied, and there was no one around to tell me to stop, so I just carried on.

I left home and made my way to the hairdresser where I met up with my bridesmaids. The hairdresser was my regular beautician, Paula. I had been using Paula for at least five years prior to my wedding day, so she was pretty familiar with my hair, the styles that suited me, and what I liked. I had already gone in a few weeks earlier to try out the style I would wear on the day. When I got there, however, Paula had a surprise for me. She got me a footrest, and she also had set up a champagne breakfast for my bridesmaids and me. It was wonderful having a champagne breakfast on my wedding day. I was totally pampered, and I loved every minute of it. Paula did my hair whilst her assistants did the bridesmaids' hair. We had plenty of time, as my wedding was at two in the afternoon.

I left my bridesmaids still getting their hair done and I made my way to Phil's parents' house. When I got there, the florist had already delivered the flowers. They were beautiful – the smell and the colours ... My bouquet was shaped something like a triangle and consisted of roses and lilies, my favourite flowers. I just loved it.

There were so many people in the house; I hated it. I just wanted peace and quiet. I found a quiet place in Phil's room, which was at the top of the house, and just hid there for a while. My maid of honour, Ruby, came and told me it was time for us to get dressed. Just then, Paula, my beautician arrived to touch up my make-up to ensure it was perfect for the pictures. I was no longer nervous. I was no longer crying. All the nerves I had felt all week seemed to have gone. I was ready for this day.

We finished dressing just as the photographer arrived. He took some beautiful shots of me inside the house. He told me how to pose. In one shot, which I particularly like, he told me to pretend to be looking out the window. The cars had now arrived. I had a white vintage Rolls Royce. It was absolutely beautiful. The photographer took some shots of me outside by the car, and some of me inside the car. By now, it seemed like everyone on the street had gathered outside to see the bride – *me!* I felt and looked like a queen. My beautician had done such a superb job with my hair and my make-up. This was it. This was my big day.

Finally, it was time to go. I was now in the car with the man I had chosen to be my father for the day. He was actually Phil's aunt's husband. He was a lovely man, and he did a great job of supporting me. I wished I had a dad even more so on this day, my wedding day! Better still, I wished I had a mother who cared about me!

I got to the church, which was on Stoke Newington High Street. Again, it seemed as if everyone stopped his or her day to take a look at the bride, to share my day! My bridesmaids were already waiting outside the church, and when I got there, they fussed around me ensuring that my long veil was set out properly and my dress was in order. Phil was already inside the church waiting for me. As I approached the church, the ushers opened up the door, and I heard the song that I had chosen to walk in to. That put a smile on my face. As I walked in, all of a sudden, it seemed as if a thousand flashbulbs went off all at once. I was blinded for a split second! I started walking with my adopted father, and I heard him telling me, 'Just smile.' And he ever so gently pulled on my arm to slow down my walking. So I flashed my whites for all the cameras as we walked slowly down the isle. If it had been left up to me, I would have been walking really fast, but my 'father' was very good at controlling the situation, and he had me walking at a slow pace so that our guests could get some pictures.

This was it! No turning back now! It was a lovely ceremony. Phil was very nervous. I was all smiles on that day. I had already done all my crying. Now that the ceremony was over, it was time to take some more photographs, only this time with my husband, my bridesmaids, Phil's groomsmen, and our guests. Would you believe the moment our wedding ceremony was finished, the heavens opened up and it started pouring in rain? I could not believe it. That did not spoil our day at all. The chauffeurs in the Rolls Royce were well trained, and they had the biggest umbrellas I had ever seen. Their job was simply to ensure that the bride did not get wet, and they certainly did a fantastic job of that.

I did not know most of the people at our wedding. They were all Phil's family. I had invited only a few cousins. My sisters and brothers were all in America, and they were still young so they had to do as Elizabeth told them.

When the photographs were all finished, it was time to go to the hall. Phil and I got into my Rolls Royce, and we made our way to the hall. The decorations were beautiful. It was really nice to walk in and see that. All our guests stood up as we entered, and we were introduced as Mr and Mrs. There was plenty of food and drink, and we were served separately. Phil and I had our own staff who catered just to us. We were very well taken care of. I was so hungry, but I just could not eat. I was totally overwhelmed.

As our guests were eating, the master of ceremony kept us entertained by introducing various guests who gave speeches. They had been instructed to keep their speeches short and sweet, which overall was adhered to. There were 350 guests at our wedding. We certainly did not send out that many invitations, but somehow I think people who were invited decided to bring along uninvited guests. Phil and I were having fun just watching everyone enjoying themselves. After we ate, it was time for Phil and I to open the dance floor! The song we danced to was 'If I had the key to the world' (L J Reynolds) It was a beautiful song. Phil and I moved on that dance floor as if we were joined together. Our movements were so smooth and so synchronized, I felt as if there was no one else there in that room but just the two of us. As we danced, I was reminded that we were not alone, as the photographer was still taking pictures, and of course, our guests were taking pictures. I was enjoying our wedding day.

It was now time for Phil and I to mingle and thank our guests for attending. It took us a while to get around to so many people. There was a time when I was all alone just for a few minutes, and the photographer took a picture of me. As I later looked back at that picture in my album, that was the one sad point of my day, because my mom was not there, and at that particular time when the photographer took that picture, I was reflecting on that loss. Every time I look at that picture, it's a painful reminder, and to make matters worse, Elizabeth did not even call!

No one seemed to want to leave our wedding. We had hired the hall only until midnight, but when that time came, people were still dancing. The after party was great. Phil's friend was a DJ on the radio, and Phil had asked him to play the music at our wedding. He was doing such a good job that no one wanted to leave. Finally at 1.30 in the morning we had to actually shut off the music to encourage folks to leave.

Finally, it was time for Phil and I to leave, but not to go home. Phil's parents had invited some of the family back to their house to party some more, and party they did. Phil and I were so tired, we ended up falling asleep in each other's arms right there on the sofa.

We had booked our honeymoon in America. We set off the next day for two weeks, and we had a ball. We took our two sons with us. We took them to Disney World, and we went to visit Phil's Aunt. She was very nice. We had a fantastic two weeks away.

For weeks after our wedding, we received thank you cards from our guests, telling us that our wedding was the best they had ever attended. Phil and I were happy, because we had put all our efforts into making our celebration a success.

THINGS GET A LITTLE ROCKY ON THE HOME FRONT

W E GOT BACK FROM OUR honeymoon and settled back into our lives. I still did not hear from Elizabeth. I again decided that I was not going to speak to her for a while. I was so mad with her. The years went by, and Phil and I both worked hard for our family. I began to notice that Phil was coming home later and later. Before, Phil would get home by 7.00 in the evening at the latest. Most nights he would be home by 5.30 to 6.00. This worked out very well, because whilst he would be bathing the boys, I would be preparing our dinner and tidying up the house. However, when he started coming home at 8.00 or 9.00, when he arrived, I would already have bathed the boys, cooked their dinner, fed them, and tidied up the house. And, worse, the boys would already be in their beds without seeing their dad. By their bedtime I was shattered every day.

Phil, on the other hand, although he was coming home late, and should be tired, did not seem tired. This was very puzzling to me. We were no longer on the same wavelength, in the bedroom in particular, because he was full of energy, and I, on the other hand, having put in a full day at work, then come home to start all over again, was exhausted. After several months of Phil coming home late, I decided to address the situation and find out exactly what was going on. I learned from Phil that the reason he was not tired when he got home, and the reason he was coming home late was that he was stopping off at his parents' home before he came home to us. He would sleep there for at least two to three hours, then he would come home. I was livid. I told him that I found his behaviour very selfish, because he had left me to do everything on my own. Not only that, but he would still expect me to function in the bedroom as well. I was really mad with his mother in particular, because she should have been able to tell him go home to his family, but she encouraged him to behave in that manner.

Phil had not seen his sons or read them a bedtime story in months. How could his mother condone this behaviour? Phil told me he was just tired, and that was why he was stopping off at his parents' house. I asked him, 'So do you not think I am tired as well?' I actually thought something was wrong with me because I could not keep up with Phil! We talked this through, and Phil apologized and promised me that it would not happen again. I believed him, and true to his word, it did not happen again for a few months. Slowly, however, I began to see the same pattern emerging again. I quickly confronted him again about this issue, and once again he would stop long enough to pacify the situation, but then he would gradually start up again.

This went on for years, and I found myself getting more and more tired, and I also found myself feeling a bit resentful towards Phil. He was so charming that, every time I would make up my mind that I was not speaking to him, he would do something really nice, and I would then forget why I was angry with him in the first place – until the next time he did it.

The years seemed to be going so fast. It was now time for my firstborn, Phil Junior, to start school. The tears flowed freely that day – my first child going to school for the first time. He had been going to nursery, but school was somehow a different ballgame. It just seemed that our little boy was so grown up. He seemed so independent. He had no problem going to school for his first day. I was the one with the problem. Phil Junior just seemed to love every bit of what was happening. He was quite a bright boy, and his teachers loved him. His teachers told us that our son had such good manners. Phil and I were very proud of him. Timothy was attending nursery, and soon it would be his turn to start school as well.

I was becoming rather concerned about Phil and our relationship. Phil was self-employed in the fashion industry, and I did everything to accommodate him. For example, every morning I would get up at 5.30 and make Phil a full cooked breakfast, which consisted of eggs, bacon, fish fingers, beef burgers, baked beans, and fried plantain along with a pot of fresh-brewed coffee. I did not eat any of this. I made it especially for Phil. I felt that Phil did not appreciate the things that I did for him, and I say this because, after eating this breakfast, Phil would just leave the plate on the worktop in the kitchen in the tray that he ate out of, and that's if he could be bothered to take it to the kitchen. Quite often he would leave the tray in the living room on the floor. At no time would he be considerate and, let's say, tidy up the kitchen.

After I made him breakfast, I would then get the boys ready for nursery and school, then I would get myself ready for my day in the office. I had no time to tidy up, but Phil did on certain days when he was not working. It was on these days that I would get very annoyed when I got home and find the kitchen exactly the same way that I had left it the morning before. This was very frustrating, because instead of coming home to get started straight away on dinner, I would first have to tidy the kitchen from the morning breakfast. I occasionally asked Phil to help me more around the house, but it just fell on deaf ears. He just would not pull his weight.

My other area of concern was that he made no time for his sons. He would never take the boys to the park. He would never kick a football around with them. In fact, he did absolutely nothing with his boys. Again, I found myself having to take on the responsibility of taking the boys to the cinema, theatre, pantomimes, and so forth, and Phil would be conveniently absent on every outing. Whenever I arranged family photographs, Phil would either show up late, or when he was on time, his eyes would be so red that there was no point including him in the pictures, so all our family pictures were just of me and the boys. I felt like a single mom in some respects.

Then there was the decorating of the house. Phil would not touch the house, so in order for the house not to be in a state of disarray, I found myself doing all the decorating. I did the painting and wall papering, and I also found myself cutting the grass and doing all the gardening work. Phil claimed he was allergic to cut grass. He did absolutely nothing around the house.

I began to grow resentful towards Phil, and I questioned if he truly loved me, because how do you love someone and then just not care about taking responsibility for your part of the chores around the house? I was so stressed out, I finally went my doctor, because I could not understand why I was just so tired all the time. We had had the same doctor for over 10 years. He knew me very well, and he asked me a few questions in order to discover why I was just so tired all the time, and why I was finding it difficult to respond to my husband the way he wanted me to. One of the questions Dr Murdoch asked was, 'What do you do around the house?' I started going down the list, and he then asked, 'What does Phil do around the house?' I told him, and his response was, 'Well, if Phil were to help you, then you would be able to …' and he stopped himself from saying anything further, but I got the point Dr Murdoch was trying to make. I felt as if I was trying to be Wonder Woman. I just never had any time to myself. I never visited friends or had a girls' night out or anything. It was just work and home for me. If I wasn't attending to the boys, I was attending to my husband. I had no *me* time. I was not particularly happy in my marriage at this stage, but I did not want my children to grow up without a father, because I had done so, and I knew just what that was like. So I decided to press my way. For better or for worse, right?

SCHOOL TIME

IT WAS NOW TIME FOR Timothy to start school. I felt so emotional watching him all dressed up in his school uniform for his first day of school, so independent and so relaxed. Again, I was the one who was a bundle of nerves. Timothy loved every minute of it. He was now attending school with his big brother. As Timothy would say, he was going to 'big boy school' now. Phil and I had decided that it was much more convenient for the boys to attend school where we lived rather than sending them to school where his parents lived. His parents did not like this decision, but we had to do what was best for the boys. We decided to get a local childminder. We found a lovely lady who lived on the next street from where we lived, so it was easy for me to drop the boys off in the mornings, and then jump on the train, which was just another street away, and go to work. This routine worked out really well.

We lived in a remote area at the time, which was not culturally developed. Apart from my two sons there were only two other black children in the whole school. Needless to say, my children were the only black children in their classes. Phil Junior would come home from school in tears and ask me why he had to be that colour. Why could he not be white like the other children? It was heartbreaking for me, so I told him that he was a special little boy sent from heaven, and that he had beautiful skin colour just like his mom and his dad. He seemed quite happy with this explanation for a while. Timothy did not get teased, because he had a light complexion like Phil's, but Phil Junior had a dark complexion like mine.

After a couple of years, our childminder decided she was going to move away out of the area. The boys loved her, and I also liked her. Phil and I decided that we did not want our boys to go to another childminder. Because of the hours I worked, and because Phil was unable to make it home on time to collect the boys from school, we decided that we would get an au pair – a person from another country who lives as part of the host family in exchange for work and a small monetary allowance. Au pairs often take a job as an opportunity to improve their language skills, and often they are students. We looked for an au pair who would do light housework and take the children to school and collect them at the end of the day. Some au pairs prepare a meal for the family as well, but I decided not to require ours to do this. The main duty would be to take care of the boys.

This arrangement turned out to be a great help for me, as Phil was never really around. It gave me peace of mind, and I did not always have to be rushing home to collect the boys after work. Additionally, when I got home, the house would be tidy. This helped out tremendously, and whilst the boys would teach the au pair English, she would teach them Spanish. We had a lovely au pairs, Suzanne, who was from Spain. The boys loved her, and she loved them. She became a part of our family, and her parents came over from Spain to meet us. We went to Spain to spend time with them also. Suzanne was like the sister I never had. We did everything together.

Having two boys always left me with a yearning for a little girl, and I believe Phil felt the same way. So in 1989, when Phil Junior was nine years old and Timothy was seven, Phil and I decided to try for another baby. We were both hoping it would be a little girl. I got pregnant almost immediately, and I knew I was pregnant straight away when I started feeling the old familiar feelings of not being able to tolerate any scented household or beauty products.

My pregnancy was confirmed, and Phil and I were elated. I was now thirty years old, and I felt great and looked great pregnant. I was much more confident than I had been at age twenty. Seven months into the pregnancy, the doctors discovered that I had toxaemia, a disease that is quite dangerous to mother and baby. I had retained a great deal of water. I was so bloated, my wedding rings had to be cut off my finger. My whole body was just swollen, and I had gone totally dark. My skin colouring had changed drastically. I had to go to the hospital every week. To make matters worse, I had developed gestational high blood pressure. Also, in the other two pregnancies, my morning sickness had stopped after three months. In this pregnancy, it just carried on throughout the whole pregnancy. Because of the excess water that I was carrying around I felt huge, but I had not put on that much weight. Even with the added complications, I had put on only one and a half stone in weight (21 pounds).

One day, later on in the pregnancy, I had not felt the baby move all day, and usually the baby had been quite active. Phil decided to take me to the hospital for a scan to find out what, if anything, was going on. When I got to the hospital, as soon as the technician placed the ultrasound probe on my stomach, the baby started moving around like crazy. It was a relief to know everything was fine.

The only problem was that, now that I was in the hospital, the doctors did not want me to go back home. They wanted me to stay, because my blood pressure was rather high. I did my best to convince them to let me go home. I told them that, if I had to stay, my blood pressure would get even higher, but if I was allowed to go home, I would just rest, and I would be okay. But they were not having any of that. They wanted me there in the hospital where they could monitor me! Oh how I hated hospitals.

Phil had taken me to the hospital on a Wednesday night. By Saturday my blood pressure, instead of going down, had gone up. I was now on complete bed rest. I hated that. The doctors decided that they were going to induce my labour. Oh, I don't think my baby liked the sound of that, and I agreed. We wanted nature to run its course. I guess, upon the shock of hearing the doctor's plans, my baby decided to be born naturally. I started feeling some pains, which I recognized as contractions. I started timing them, and they were about half an hour apart. I then had a show, which was another sign that I was in active labour. When the midwife checked me, I was four centimetres dilated. The contractions were getting stronger. Then, all of a sudden, the contractions stopped.

It was now Sunday evening, and I'd had no contractions all day, but the good news was that my blood pressure had gone down. I was no longer on bed rest. Several of my friends told me that, if I walked around, I might be able to get my labour started again. I decided to take their advice, and I went for a walk around the wards. To my surprise, I started feeling contractions again. They were very strong and about a half an hour apart again.

Phil and I had already decided that we would not have any more children, so I wanted to experience natural childbirth. When the contractions were about three minutes apart, I did question my decision. The pain was excruciating, so I asked for some pain relief and was given a pethidine injection in the leg. I was also given gas and air. I sucked on that air so fast. The nurses tried telling me to go slower, but I was just not hearing that at the time.

Little Ethan came into the world weighing a healthy six pounds one ounce. Yes, you guessed it, another boy. Ethan was absolutely beautiful. Again, like his two brothers, he was white like a Caucasian baby. He had a mop of straight, black hair, and he had long fingers. He was very sleepy, and the nurses said it was because of the gas and air that I had inhaled.

No sooner had I delivered Ethan than I started being sick. Again, too much gas and air. It pays to listen, but in my defence, I was just in too much pain to even comprehend what the nurses were saying, let alone put their advice into action, but I sure paid the price.

Ethan was such a gorgeous baby. Here I was again feeling that love that only a mother knows! Phil was sitting next to me in shock with his mouth wide open, because he just could not believe that he had another son. A month before Ethan was born, I had a dream in which I saw that I had given birth to a baby boy, and I told Phil about that dream at the time, but I guess he'd just dismissed it. I had also told Phil I felt as if I was carrying a boy, because all the symptoms from the other two pregnancies were exactly the same except for the extended morning sickness.

Because Ethan was our last child, I decided that I wanted to spend as much time with him as possible, so I had stayed at work for as long as I was able to, then I stayed home with Ethan until he was six months old before I went back to work. Suzanne, our au pair, was superb with Ethan. She just adored him, so I made her his godmother.

Ethan was growing up into a lovely boy, but he seemed to be always sick. He would start off with a high temperature, and he would not be able to keep anything down, so he would end up in the hospital, as his fever would be so high. I could not even get him to take the medication to lower his temperature. As soon as he would see the spoon coming to his mouth, he would start being sick. Once the hospital staff were able to get his temperature under control, he would be released, usually after a few days. We had learnt that Ethan had enlarged adenoids. They acted as sponges, just picking up viruses and colds and fevers constantly. Ethan was actually on permanent antibiotics. He had to take the medication every day to prevent him from getting even sicker, as he was too young to have surgery on his adenoids. The doctors informed us that he would have to wait until he was two years old.

I also noticed that, although Ethan was a very happy baby and he was developing normally, he was losing his hair. I took him to the doctor, who referred him to a specialist paediatrician. This paediatrician did not seem bothered about the hair loss, but it bothered me. Ethan was allergic to regular milk, so I had been told to give him only soy milk. Having had two children before, I was experienced enough to know that there was just something that bothered me about Ethan. I could not quite place my finger on it, but I knew something was not right with him. Every month I was taking him to the paediatrician and voicing my concerns, but I was being treated like an overly concerned mother who did not know what she was talking about. I was watching my child losing his hair, and I had to take action.

During my next visit to the paediatrician, I again voiced my concerns and I was again fobbed off. This time I was not having it. I looked the paediatrician straight in the eyes and demanded that he refer Ethan to a consultant immediately. I would not leave until it was done. I guess the paediatrician knew that I meant it; he had never seen me like that before. Straight away he wrote the letter and referred me to a consultant to be seen immediately – the next day. She was a lovely lady. Liliian fell in love with Ethan, who by now had some bald patches on his head. When she ran some tests, she found out that Ethan was suffering from malnutrition. In addition, he had oesophageal reflux. As a baby, whenever Ethan ate, he would always throw up his food. It is normal for young babies to do this, but as Ethan grew older, the condition did not stop. Sometimes he would just shoot his sickness across the room. How could my child be suffering from malnutrition in this day and age? I was surely feeding him well, so how could this be? He seemed fine on the outside. In fact, every health professional had told me I was over-exaggerating my concerns.

A mother usually knows when something is not right with her child. Every week I would go to the health food store and spend a small fortune buying the week's supply of soy milk for Ethan. What I hadn't been told, however, was that the soy milk I was buying was not fortified for a baby. His milk should actually have been prescribed by the doctor. I might as well have been giving Ethan a glass of water as give him the soy milk that I had been buying. That, coupled with the oesophageal reflux, meant that Ethan was absorbing absolutely no nutrients in his little body. I was furious, because the doctor who told me to give Ethan soy milk should have been prescribing the milk all along. My child could have died had I not put my foot down that day.

I had so many sleepless nights with Ethan. He was in the hospital at least once a month. I had lost count of the number of times I would leave from the hospital and go straight to work. I was fortunate enough that I worked for a company that had established core hours between 10.00 a.m. and 4.00 p.m., so whenever Ethan was in the hospital, I would simply do the core hours and would make up the time afterwards.

Ethan had stopped breathing a couple of times. I actually thought we were going to lose him. The hospital was fantastic; they actually sent two nurses to our home to teach Phil and I how to perform CPR in case Ethan stopped breathing again.

Knowing Ethan's frailty, Phil and I decided to take him from Faye, Phil's mom. This was a hard decision, because she was really the best person to care for Ethan, but on the other hand, there were times when Ethan was sick and I could not get to him for an hour and a half, and in Ethan's case, this could be quite dangerous. Once I was speeding to get to Ethan, and I was caught by the police and given a ticket. Ethan tended to have high temperatures, which, if not treated promptly, could result in him having a fit, which I just could not risk. Phil's mom did not drive, and furthermore, even if she did, she had other children that she was taking care of. We decided to have him at a childminder close to my work. The new childminder was a two-minute drive away from where I worked. She was the wife of one of my work colleagues. Her name was Regina. She was white, and she adored Ethan. Ethan was just so adorable, you couldn't help but love him. He had big, brown eyes and eyelashes so long people were inspired to comment on them.

One day Regina took Ethan into the town centre of Hertfordshire where I worked, which was predominantly a white area, and Ethan started being sick. He had problems breathing. Regina was CPR qualified; I had made sure of that. She was holding Ethan face down and patting him on his back firmly. She got quite scared, because a crowd of people were gathering around her. They thought she was abusing Ethan. She had to quickly explain to them what she was doing.

Time seemed to be going very quickly, and soon Ethan was two years old. He was now scheduled for the surgery to have his adenoids removed. Phil and I took Ethan to the hospital. I felt so helpless as they took him away for surgery. All I could do was to pray. He was now in God's hands. The surgery seemed to take forever. In reality it was only a half an hour. The procedure went well, and Ethan was fine. Phil and I stayed at the hospital with our son until he woke up. I stayed the night, and Phil went home to take care of Phil Junior and Timothy. The next day, Ethan's brothers came to see him. We were able to take Ethan home after a week. Right from the start after the surgery there was something different about Ethan. We no longer had to give him daily antibiotics, and he did not get sick anymore. The first sick-free month went by, and then another and another. It was fantastic. It was truly the first time since Ethan was born that three months had gone by without him being sick. The months turned into years, and Ethan was absolutely fine. The doctors had been right after all. They always told us that, when Ethan's adenoids were removed, he would be fine. It had been difficult to take on board at the time, but now it was finally happening.

A Bit of a Rough Time

I HAD NOTICED THAT WHENEVER PHIL needed to be around at the important times in the children's lives, he would always be there. But he was often absent for family time. I actually call that social time. He was always too busy, and as a result, by the time Phil Junior was twelve years old, Timothy was ten, and Ethan was two, Phil had never taken his sons to the park or played ball with them in the garden. He was still on the same routine – up early, home late, and never coming home in time to put his sons to bed or even to read them a story. I had long given up on asking him to do those things. I would do all of that, and with Suzanne around the pressure was off Phil.

Somehow, Phil thought that as long as he provided financially, that was all that his family needed. I just could not seem to make him understand that we needed *him*, not just money. We, as a family, needed *him*.

Suzanne was really good with the boys, and she would often read them bedtime stories. She made my life a lot easier. I felt that I had that little bit more time to myself. I needed some me time so badly. I felt that I was now more able to respond to my husband, and of course he was loving all the attention. Life was good. Suzanne had been with us for over two years and had informed us that it was now time for her to go home to Spain, as she had completed her studies. I would surely miss her, and so would the boys.

On hearing this, I decided to change my job. I did not want to work in Hertfordshire anymore. I wanted to work locally and be close to the boys in case of emergencies. There was a job being advertised which was ten minutes away from home, and the money, when I worked it out, was pretty much the same as what I was earning currently. I applied and got the job, and I was ecstatic.

I had been at this company for two years, and I really liked it. I had been feeling a pain in my side on and off for about a year, and my doctor had told me that I had a grumbling appendix. I was at work one Friday when this pain became very severe. I started being sick, but I just decided to stick it out, as it was Friday. I did not want to take any time off work and go home sick, so I stayed at work not telling anyone I was feeling unwell. As I was driving home, I decided to call my doctor, as the pain was still severe. The receptionist answered the phone, and when I asked to speak to my doctor, she informed me that he was already in surgery. The receptionist enquired if there was anything she could help me with. I told her that I had a pain in my side, and before I could say another word, I was speaking to Dr Murdoch. He asked me to describe the pain and asked if I had been sick. He seemed concerned and asked me if I was able to make it to the surgery. I was confused as to why he would ask me if I was able to drive to the surgery, but I was about to find out. When I got there, although he had a waiting room full of patients, Dr Murdoch saw me immediately, and when he examined me, he pressed my side and I screamed and doubled up in the foetal position. He dialled 999 himself, and the next thing I knew, I was in an ambulance going to Chase Farm Hospital. I was scheduled for surgery immediately for an emergency appendectomy.

I was told that, if I had not gone to the doctor that evening, and had gone home and taken some painkillers like I had planned to, I would have died in my sleep from a ruptured appendix. Phil called my workplace on the Monday to inform them that I'd had to have emergency surgery on the Friday evening, and they did not believe him. They told Phil I had been at work on Friday and I had been perfectly fine. It was not until Phil took in the doctor's certificate that they believed I was in the hospital. I received a huge basket of flowers and a huge card signed by everyone in my office. It really cheered me up. Oddly, it was years later after I had left this company that I learned that the receptionist, Joy, actually died in her sleep from a ruptured appendix. Joy had done what I'd been about to do on that Friday evening. She'd taken some painkillers and gone to bed, and her husband found her passed away in bed. Joy was such a beautiful person, but she is now a beautiful angel.

When I had my appendix out, the surgeons made a large incision. This was before the days of keyhole, or laparoscopic, surgery. I was in the hospital for two weeks. I had no idea of what was to come. After the surgery, I sank into a deep depression. It was a kind of depression that I never even knew existed; neither had I seen it coming. I had the best doctor in the world. I never even knew that I was depressed. I went to see Doctor Murdoch for my two-week check, and without warning I just burst into tears and just could not stop crying. This was very uncharacteristic of me.

By this time, I had known my doctor for ten years, and he had never seen me cry, so he knew something was up with me. After that, whenever I booked an appointment, at Dr Murdoch's instruction, I would book the last appointment of the day, and he would spend hours counselling me. I thought I had gotten over the rape, but I had never told anyone about the rape apart from Phil, and I did not really share the details with Phil – just the basics. I had never received counselling. So here I was, at thirty-two years old, being counselled for something that had happened nineteen years ago. I felt like such a fool, but I just could not get the experience out of my head. At the time, I just felt that I needed to go into details and tell someone what Mr Nash had done to me. I called it telling the dirty bits. Once I was able to do this, I went through several months of counselling before I could feel at peace about this again.

My doctor told me that the sudden trauma of the surgery had bought on the depression. It was good having my family around me, because they certainly helped me on the road to recovery. I finally reached a stage in my recovery that took me from depression to anger. Several times every day I would just feel such a rage come over me that I found it difficult to contain myself. We were not busy at work on one particular day, and I was sitting at my desk cleaning my keyboard whilst plotting how I could get back at Mr Nash for what he did to me. I was plotting in my mind that I was going to get a gun, and I was going to smuggle it out to Jamaica. I would go searching for Mr Nash, then I would use the gun to shoot him and kill him.

Only first I would be sure to remind him of who I was and what he had done to me. He needed to pay for what he had done to me, and perhaps to many more young girls like myself!

All of a sudden, I heard a voice very clearly saying, 'Thank Him for the pain.' I looked at my colleague next to me, and I said to her, 'What did you say?' She looked at me, stunned, and said, 'I did not say anything!' I already knew she hadn't, but there was no one else around, and I needed to be clear on what I was hearing. I started cleaning the keyboard again, and I heard the voice clearly again saying to me, 'Thank Him for the pain.' I then recognized the voice to be the same voice that I had heard in my mind many times before, only this time the voice was audible. At the same time, I felt an incredible peace, and I just found myself sitting right there at my desk, with tears flowing, just saying, 'Thank you, Lord, for the pain.' I said it over and over again. From that day to this, I have never felt the need to seek revenge on Mr Nash, because I know that God will take care of Mr Nash for me. The word of the Lord says, '"Vengeance is Mine, I will repay," says the Lord' (Hebrews 10:30 New King James Version). To this day, I still carry this peace with me, and it has helped to complete my healing process.

MEETING SEMONA-JANE

THE YEARS FLEW BY. ETHAN was now in school, and both his brothers were now in secondary school. Throughout the years, I had always gone to church, and Phil Junior and Timothy were brought up in church. But after my surgery, I had not gone back to church for at least two years. I had everything I needed, but I felt an emptiness. I felt like a fish out of water. I wanted Ethan to go to church, and I found a Sunday school for him to attend. It was so convenient, because the Sunday school operators would pick Ethan up from home and drop him back off after Sunday school. This worked well for a while. Ethan loved it, but then he started kicking up a fuss, saying that he did not want to go to Sunday school.

I had always brought my children up under the conviction that I would never ask them to do something I was not prepared to do myself. So here I was being put to the test. I needed to start going back to church. It was very difficult, and week after week I would make excuses not to go. But eventually I made it back to church. I felt such a peace. It was as if the church experience was filling the void that I had felt. Not surprisingly, Ethan now loved going to Sunday school.

Phil was not a churchgoer. He did not like church. His family never attended church, but I had been brought up in the church, and I loved it. I soon made new friends. One such friend was a young lady called Semona-Jane. I did not like Semona-Jane at first. I found her to be quite aggressive, and I stayed away from her. I found her to be very domineering, and I did not like that about her. At the same time, I had a friend called Janine, and Janine was a good friend of Semona-Jane's. One day I was speaking with Janine when she mentioned that Semona-Jane was okay. She suggested that I get to know her, because she had just moved to London and did not have any friends there. Semona-Jane had been trying to be friends with me, but I had just been avoiding her, and I was not being friendly back because I just did not like her demeanour. However, Janine was a good friend of mine, and feeling a bit guilty about how I had been pushing Semona-Jane away, I decided to try to be Semona-Jane's friend.

The next time I had a conversation with Semona-Jane, instead of just giving her the yes or no answers I had given her in the past, I started to warm to her. She seemed like a nice person, and when I started getting to know her, I realized that she was not that bad. I was still sceptical, however, and took my time to get to know her. I introduced Semona-Jane to my family, and none of my children liked her; neither did Phil. I had never experienced that before. Usually my children liked my friends, and so did Phil. I just put it down to the fact that I did not have many friends, and because I was actually going out and doing things, they did not like her because they saw her as a bad influence on me.

Semona-Jane was unmarried and did not have a boyfriend. She worked as a counsellor, but she was also a psychologist. Semona-Jane and I talked quite a lot on the phone. As well, we would meet up once a week for a girls' night out. This was all new to me. Phil, on the other hand, all throughout our marriage, had always had his boys' night out during the week, and on a Friday night he would play dominoes with his friends. Phil did not like the fact that I was actually getting out of the house and doing things. He liked me to always be at home, and wanted me to cancel my girls' night out. I explained to him that this was not fair, because he had other interests outside our marriage, and it was time that I developed some interests of my own. He really did not like it, but he decided to go along with the idea. So as not to interfere with Phil's night outs, which were usually on Wednesdays, I decided to have my girls' night out on Thursdays. Phil would babysit Ethan when the boys were not going to be home. He hated it, but Ethan loved it, because he got some alone time with his daddy, and they really developed a close bond.

One night Semona-Jane asked me, 'So when do you and your husband spend alone time together as a couple? When do you have your special night out?' *Special night out ... alone time together ... what is she talking about?* I thought. *Phil and I haven't done that in years.* During the early years of our marriage we did, but as time went by, we simply did not go out together anymore. As a matter of fact, I had totally forgotten what that was like. I told her that we didn't have any special time together. She was alarmed. She asked what we did as a couple. Again, I told her nothing.

Semona-Jane asked what Phil did for a job and what time he got home. I told her that he came home quite late. She said she did not feel that his time was spent working. Phil sometimes came home at 10.00 or 11.00 in the evening, and he would tell me that he had been out buying. Semona-Jane said, 'Which shop do you know that is open until those hours in the night?' She had a point; I did not know of any. I quickly jumped to Phil's defence as I had been with Phil on numerous occasions when he would actually go to a supplier's home to pick up goods late at night, although not usually later than 7.00. I explained this to Semona, but she was not convinced.

Semona had me thinking. You see, it had started off very subtly with Phil coming home late, and it just escalated to the point where I just accepted it as normal. Phil used to be home every evening between 6.00 and 7.00. Then the time slowly changed to 8.00. For example, every Friday night Phil would come home, and we would take the boys out to eat – pizza or Chinese or whatever we fancied. Then Phil started coming home later, so we decided that, as he came home so late, we would have the food delivered. We were still having a take-away and eating together once a week as a family. Then Phil started coming home even later, so the only place that was still open was a well-known fried chicken restaurant, so the boys and I would welcome fried chicken every Friday night. Then Phil began coming home so late that not even this restaurant was an option anymore.

I still did not take on any negativity that Semona-Jane was try-ing to throw my way. I knew my Phil. How dare she insinuate that my husband was not telling the truth! Who did she think she was? Somehow, although I was angry with Semona-Jane, I did see some truth in what she was saying. I knew she was suggesting that Phil was having an affair, but I was having none of her ideas. After all, when

Phil had that affair earlier on in our marriage, he had promised me faithfully that he would never do it again, and I believed him. Surely he would never do that to me again a second time? Would he?

From then on Semona-Jane set out to prove to me that Phil was indeed having an affair. One day, Phil had taken my car as he often did on a Wednesday when he was not working. Phil would usually rest on Wednesdays. I worked quite close to where Semona-Jane worked, so she was giving me a ride home from work. As we entered into my road, Phil was coming out of our road in my car, but he was in such a hurry! We were right next to him, and I was waving at him, but he did not see us. He knew Semona-Jane's car, but he seemed so preoccupied that he did not even see us. Semona-Jane said, 'Let's follow him.' I said, *'No!'* But she said, 'I am going to prove to you that your husband is having an affair.' So Semona-Jane turned the car around and began to follow Phil. I was not proud of myself, but I needed to know if she was right. We followed Phil to an area I was not familiar with. Phil and I certainly had no mutual friends living in that area, and he had never spoken of any of his friends living there. All of a sudden Phil indicated to pull into a space. So as not to let him know that we were following him, Semona-Jane continued to drive. Then she quickly turned the car around, and we came back on ourselves just in time to see Phil putting a key into a front door. He opened the door and went inside. Because we could not stop, and we had to keep driving, we did not see the number of the door that he had entered.

I was in such denial, I told Semona-Jane that I believed that Phil was trying to surprise me. I told her I believed that Phil had bought that house, and he was remodelling it. He would surprise me when he was finished. I was just not willing even for one minute to accommodate the very idea that Phil was having an affair. He wouldn't cheat on me again, oh no, not my Phil. *No! No! No!* We drove back home in silence, and Semona-Jane dropped me off and went home. I sat at home with all kinds of thoughts going through my head, waiting for Phil to return home. He did not get home until 10.30 that night. Although I had seen Phil go into a house using a key, I did not know the number of the house that he had entered.

The next Wednesday, I decided to drive back to where I had seen Phil park our car. This time I got there before he did, and I parked in the side road facing the houses. This paid off. Sure enough, Phil pulled up in his van, and I noted the number of the house that Phil, once again, entered using his very own key.

BUSINESS TRIP

SOON AFTER I DISCOVERED PHIL going into the strange house with his key, he informed me that he was going away on a business trip to Bulgaria. I found this strange, because in all the years we had been together, Phil had gone away only once on business. This trip had been with his former business partner to Bangkok in Thailand. I had packed his suitcase, and his partner had sorted out the travel arrangements. I had been involved every step of the way.

This trip felt very different. Phil, as far as I knew, did not know anyone in Bulgaria. He certainly had never mentioned Bulgaria before. He was very secretive about the arrangements, and he insisted on packing his own case. At the same time, there was a conference in Atlanta, Georgia, in the United States, that was being conducted by T.D. Jakes called Woman Thou Art Loosed. A group of five ladies in the church decided we wanted to go, as it promised to be very powerful. I asked Phil if I could go, and he said yes. I had never been away without Phil before.

Phil would be away for two weeks on his business trip; the day he returned home was the day I would be leaving for the T.D. Jakes conference. We would actually pass each other mid flight. This meant that we would not actually see each other for a whole month.

Phil's suitcase was packed, but there were no business clothes in the suitcase; all I saw in the case were all the holiday clothes I had bought for him for our own holidays. Bulgaria is a cold country, but all Phil had packed were vests and shorts. I thought that was strange. Also, I did not see his ticket anywhere. All very strange.

The day he was to leave on his business trip, Phil asked me to give him a lift to the station so he could get the train to the airport. 'Of course I will give you a ride to the station,' I said. But I had no intention of dropping Phil off at the station. I drove our car to the railway station, and I proceeded to park up the car. Phil looked as if he was about to have a heart attack. 'What are you doing?' he asked in a high-pitched voice, filled with anger. I said, 'I am coming to the airport to see my husband off.' He said, 'You can't do that!' I said, 'Why not? You are my husband, and it is my duty to see you off.' He yelled, 'I won't buy your train ticket!' I said, 'That's okay, honey, I have my own money, so I will buy my own ticket.' Phil was so mad with me. He bought a newspaper, and he did not speak to me for the whole journey. He held the newspaper to hide his face the entire journey, which took an hour.

When we got to the airport, I looped my arm in his much to his annoyance, and I would not let him out of my sight at all. It was time for Phil to check in, and when he joined the queue, I saw old ladies wearing straw hats; everyone was dressed in summer clothes. I looked up at the checking-in desk. The sign above said Antigua. I looked at Phil, and I said to him, 'This is a funny-looking Bulgaria.' He looked at me and smiled sheepishly – the kind of smile that said, 'Okay, you caught me.' I knew then that Phil was not travelling alone. I looked all around the terminal to see if I could see an unattached female, but I did not, so I guessed that, when his woman had seen me, she had made herself scarce. You see, she had the advantage, because she knew what I looked like. I did not know what she looked like.

Phil did not even like taking a family holiday, let alone a holiday to Antigua, a country he had never been to. He would never go alone! No way.

Phil had also been telling me that he had been going out to clubs on Saturday nights, or parties. I found that strange, because we had always gone to such places together. What was even stranger was that, whenever Phil came back from his so-called club or party, I would discover that it must have just been a club or a party for two. I came to this conclusion because his clothes never smelled of smoke, or that nightclub smell. His shirts would not even be creased. They would be as fresh as a daisy. It was literally as if he had just worn the shirt for a brief period of time then taken it off. I was later to confirm this when, one such Saturday night, I decided to follow Phil to see which club he was visiting. The club or party he was visiting was right there at that woman's house. I sat there for a while and watched my husband and his woman. My heart was breaking to see my husband and another woman together!

When I got back from the T.D. Jakes conference, I came into our home and was welcomed warmly by the boys. Phil, on the other hand, was a bit cold. I had not seen my husband for a month, and he was as cold as could be. He put on the usual pretence for the sake of the boys, I guessed. We started to watch a movie, and I was talking about my trip, but Phil had nothing to say about his trip. At 10.00 p.m., when the movie was finished, Phil got up and announced to us that he was going out. My initial reaction was to burst into tears. I had just got back home, and my husband was going out. I knew exactly where he was going. At this point, Phil got up and started hugging me. 'If you want me to stay, I will stay,' he said. 'I won't go.' But it was too late. I now knew what was in his heart.

I went into the kitchen and got a tissue and quickly dried my eyes, scolding myself for being so vulnerable in front of Phil. How could I let him see how much this was really hurting me? *You silly woman*, I told myself! I quickly composed myself, and I told Phil to go. I would be just fine. After all, I had gotten used to being on my own. Sometimes Phil would even come home at 5.00 in the morning. He would come home, start hugging me and kissing me, just generally being all over me. But I would refuse his advances. He would then get showered and go to work.

He would tell me stories; for example, his best friend was sick, and he was staying with him to take care of him. This all sounded very noble, but why would he want to take care of a grown man who was married and had a family of his own? Another favourite story was that he had to stay with his sister Dreema, because he had to protect her from her boyfriend. Really, Phil? I knew these were all lies, but I was just giving him enough rope to hang himself.

That night, Phil said, 'Are you sure you are going to be okay?' I said, 'Yes, I'll be just fine.' By this time I knew three different routes to get to this woman's house, so I sat down long enough to give Phil enough time to get there and to make himself comfortable. I then called Timothy, who was at this time eighteen years old. I pulled one of Phil's shirts from the dirty linen basket, and I said to Timothy, 'Smell this shirt and tell me, does this smell like a shirt that's been worn to a club?' Timothy said, 'No!' I then told him what had been happening. I told him where I was going, and I asked him if he wanted to come along. He said no he didn't want to. I then asked him to babysit Ethan.

I jumped in my car and drove myself to this woman's house. I had now been watching Phil have this affair with this woman for over three months. I had not told him that I knew his every move. Some nights, I would just drive to the house and watch their movements through the windows. One night I wanted something from my car, and Phil had driven my car to her house, so I used my keys to get into my car, which was parked right outside her house. I took out the item that I needed, locked the car, and went back home!

I made several trips to that house on nights when Phil had told me that he would be out buying. I had to know what was going on in my marriage, so many nights, I would just take a ride up to the house, just to check if Phil's van was there. Each and every time, sure enough, his van would be parked right there outside that woman's house. On another occasion, when Phil left home, I decided to take a drive by that woman's house. I found that the curtains were not drawn. I was parked in the street directly facing the house. I saw my husband walk up the stairs with that woman, and I watched them undress and start kissing before they drew the curtains. Still on another occasion, early one morning, at around three o'clock, I was unable to sleep, so I decided to take a drive down to that woman's house. As I got there, I saw the bedroom lights go on, and I saw the silhouette of Phil getting dressed. I watched him as he came down the stairs. He was driving his van, which was not as quick as my Mercedes. I quickly took one of the other routes I knew. I got myself home and quickly tucked myself into bed as if I had not moved all night long.

What was so disgusting to me was that, whenever Phil came home from that woman's house, he would be all over me. He would come into our bed, and he would start trying to kiss me, and he would try to make love to me. How could he? Was this some sort of guilt to cover his tracks? Or was he not being satisfied? I was not about to find out, as the moment I discovered that Phil was having an affair, I had constant really bad headaches each time he would make an advance to me. I was not about to suffer the same fate as I had previously suffered from his other affair.

THE CONFRONTATION

As I mentioned earlier, Phil played dominoes on Friday nights with his friends. One Friday night, I decided to take a drive to the hall where Phil was supposedly playing with his friends. To my surprise, he had not been there for weeks, and that Friday night the session was in full swing; Phil was nowhere to be seen. I called Phil whilst standing outside the domino hall, and again, he informed me that he was at the hall playing dominoes. I asked him if it was the same place he always played, and he confirmed that it was. I made him none the wiser that I was right there and he wasn't. *It's time to face the music, Phil!*

I arrived at that woman's house. You can see that I call her 'that woman' because I have no respect for her. She knew Phil was married and had a family, and she went after him anyway. I knew this because she was a hairdresser, and one of her clients just happened to be my friend. She had confided in my friend that she had met a man who was married and had three boys. His wife was in the church. This woman actually knew me!

I walked up to the front door and rang the doorbell. A very dark-skinned woman with a glow to her skin – you know the glow you get when you have been on holiday – came to the window. She had nothing on, but she had pulled a duvet across herself to hide her nakedness. I sat on the wall and made myself comfortable and waited for my husband to get dressed. When Phil got to the door and saw me, he said, 'I knew you would follow me here one day. I mean you can see what's been happening here. I will admit I have been sleeping with her, but it's you I want. I don't want her! You were never meant to find out about this!'

He was standing on his lover's doorstep saying these words to me. I looked at him and I said, 'You are nothing but dirt. You're under my feet. You two deserve each other. Don't ever touch me. Don't speak to me. Don't ever come near me again. I don't ever want to see you or have anything else to do with you again!' I never once even raised my voice at him. With that said, I turned and walked back to my car.

Phil ran behind me telling me to wait. I got into the car and locked the door. He pulled on the door trying to open it, and then he tapped on the window trying to get me to open the window. I was totally finished with Phil. I drove off and left him standing there. I went home and proceeded to empty his wardrobes and his drawers. I packed every piece of clothing he owned in black bags and put them in the garage for him.

The next morning, Phil came home and went into our bedroom. I guessed he was looking for a change of clothes. He was beside himself. 'What have you done? What have you done?' he repeated over and over again. What had *I* done? Should that not have been the question he should have asked himself? You see, Phil wanted to have his cake and eat it too, but I was done being a doormat. How could he deface his Monet? All his promises were just lies, pure lies. It may have taken me a while to see through the lies, and I may never have seen through them had it not been for Semona-Jane, but now that I knew what Phil was up to, I was finished with my marriage. I was not about to sit around again and listen to some more promises of 'I will never do that again' only, years later, to discover that he was up to his old tricks. As far as I was concerned, Phil was making promises that he was incapable of keeping. I would no longer be a part of this sham of a marriage.

How long had he been having this affair? I had watched him for three months, but exactly how long has it been going on? How many other affairs had Phil had throughout the course of our marriage? I guessed I would never know, and to be totally honest, at this point I did not care to know. Had there ever been just the two of us in our marriage, or had it always been three people?

USER

S EMONA-JANE HAD BEEN RIGHT! AT this stage, I had very mixed
feelings about Semona-Jane, but had it not been for her, I would
never have known what Phil was up to out there. Would I have
found out eventually? Probably. Who knows? Did Semona-Jane do
it with the right motives? Of course not. She set out to prove a point
knowing very well that it would destroy my marriage, and I was too
naive to see this. I actually thought that Semona-Jane loved and cared
for me, but I was sadly mistaken. She was a user and a home breaker.
The fact that my entire family did not like her should have been
warning enough for me, but I thought she was my best friend. I even
adopted her as my sister. Big mistake. She took me for everything
that she could get from me! I loved Semona-Jane so much. I could
not even see that she was using me.

Semona-Jane did not have a car, and for two years I picked her
up every single morning and drove her to work. I had to pass her
workplace to get to mine. I worked less than ten minutes from where
she worked, and we lived less than ten minutes away from each other.
Semona-Jane would take my car every day. She would drop me to
work and take my car, and then pick me up in the evenings. Her
job demanded that she have a car, as she often had to make visits to
client's homes, and she had various other duties that required a car.
I lent her my car each day. Every week I would fill up my car with
petrol, and Semona-Jane would use it all up and would not replace it.
I started asking Semona-Jane to contribute to the petrol after about
a year, as she was the one who used my car the most. As a matter of
fact, some nights when Semona-Jane had to go out, she would ask to
borrow my car, and then she would pick me up in the morning for
work. She drove my car much more than I did, so much so that peo-

ple thought that my car belonged to her. She actually had a problem contributing to the petrol, so much so that many times I would just fill up my car without her contributing. I could not be bothered with the sarcastic comments and the feelings of belittlement that would come from her.

I remember that, at one point, the car needed some repair work done, and Semona-Jane told me she would contribute half of the money towards the repair. To date I am still waiting to receive that payment. Finally, after two years, Semona-Jane bought a car. I was so elated. I would get my Mercedes back! I would have no one dictating to me what music I could and could not listen to, or at what volume. I was so excited, I went and had my car valeted inside and out. Semona-Jane did not much care to clean my car, and if she spilled drinks, she would just leave it, and the stain would settle in.

To my total dismay, because Semona-Jane did not want to buy the road tax for her vehicle, her new car sat in her drive for a whole month while I still picked her up, and she still used my car each day. Finally, she decided to tax her vehicle. You would have thought I would be the first person that Semona-Jane would offer a ride to in her new car. Oh, no. I was not even invited for a drive at all. It was months before I actually got into her car, and that was because we were going somewhere, and she happened to be driving! I think the straw that broke the camel's back for me was the day she ignored my youngest son, Ethan. He was walking, and he saw my car approaching him. He thought, *Yes, my mom! I'm going to get a ride home!* Semona-Jane looked right at him and drove past him, leaving him to walk whilst she drove my car. How dare she?

There are a lot of women out there who are living a lie in their marriages, and I was one of those women. Even in the early part of our relationship, I never felt loved. I did not know it then, but being older and wiser, I have learnt that love is an action word. Jesus said he loves us, and He gave His life to show us that He loves us. So if a man says, 'I love you', and he truly means it, then he should be prepared to go above and beyond for you. There was only one place I felt warmth from Phil, and that was in the bedroom. And looking back now, from where I am coming from, I realize that I would have interpreted any form of affection as love. It's sad to say, but the bed-room was the only place in my marriage that I felt loved. Phil did not show me love otherwise.

I should have picked up on these things years earlier, but I guess I was just too busy raising our kids. For example, on occasions such as Mothers' Day or my birthday, Phil would buy me flowers, but he would never hand them to me. I would just find them lying on the dining table. I would just pick them up and put them in a vase with water, grateful that he had bought me flowers. On birthdays, he would buy me a card that would say, 'to my dear wife' or words to that effect, but he could not be bothered to write in the card, and I would just be grateful that he'd got me a card. You see, I had no one to tell me that this was not right. I thought this was the way it was meant to be. Now, when I look back, I realize that Phil was just going through the motions.

You may be wondering how I could function in this manner, but I had never had a male role model to show me how things should be done between a man and a woman. All I grew up seeing was my mother and my stepfather fighting each other – and I mean physical fighting and cursing. On one such occasion, Elizabeth was dressed in a beautiful brown suit, and she was going to church, but her husband did not want her to go to church. They had a fight right there in our front yard with spectators watching. I decided right there and then that, when I grew up and got married, I would not do the things I saw Elizabeth do to her husband. Every time Elizabeth had an argu-ment with her husband, she would refuse to cook for him or wash his clothes. I decided my life would not be like that, so Phil and I never really argued. We would have heated discussions at times, but we never really argued.

Phil never raised his hands to me. He was never physically abu-sive, but he was mentally abusive. An example of such behaviour occurred when I had our third son. I was only a size twelve, and I had just given birth to our son. I weighed 140 pounds. Phil turned around and said to me, 'If anyone had told me you would be so fat, I would have said, "Never in a million years".' My self-esteem was on the floor. He stopped telling me I was beautiful; he stopped telling me he loved me. In fact, I really thought I was quite ugly when I was with Phil. I had always been a size 8 to 10, and Phil told me I was too fat to wear tops with spaghetti straps, and he said I did not have a good enough figure to wear jeans.

When I left Phil, I discovered the real me. Phil and I got married young, but we did not grow together. We grew apart, because I believe that, at any given time, there were three people in our marriage. I will always love Phil, because he is the father of my children, and I will always give him that respect. I don't believe Phil is a bad person. I just believe he was very misguided.

I was with Phil for twenty-two years of my life. Now we don't even speak. We were best friends, not just husband and wife. I lost my best friend, my husband, and my lover all at the same time. I don't know when I fell out of love with Phil, or more to the point when Phil fell out of love with me, but there is a Jamaican saying that goes like this: 'Every day you carry a bucket to the well, one day the bottom must fall out.' I guess with Phil being absent over the years, with all of his lies and mental abuse, somewhere along the line I just fell out of love!

Although Semona-Jane was a home breaker, she made me know I was a beautiful woman. She boosted my self-esteem and my confidence. She made me know I was somebody! She stuck by me at what proved to be one of the most difficult times in my life, even though she had been the instigator. For that I am grateful, although her motives were not right. She taught me a lot about make-up, shopping for clothes, and making the best of myself. She brought out my best qualities, some of which I did not even know I had. You see when I was with Phil, because Phil was in the clothing industry, he did not like me buying clothes. Instead, he would always bring me the clothes he wanted me to wear. I never really shopped for clothes. Semona-Jane taught me about the type of clothes that suited my body type – clothes that would accentuate my figure, because the clothes I was accustomed to wearing were not very flattering. They mostly hid my figure. She taught me how to conduct myself as a lady where men were concerned. I learnt a lot from Semona-Jane, both good and bad. At times she was like the devil in hell, and at other times she could be the sweetest person I knew, but as I mentioned earlier, Semona-Jane was a psychologist, and she loved playing mind games with people. She was very good at twisting a person's words to make them sound the way she wanted them to. At times I was left wondering if I was going crazy! The sad thing was that playing with people's minds was all a game for Semona-Jane. I have heard it said that some people are in your life for a season, and some people are meant to stay in your life forever. I believe that Semona-Jane was one of those people who was meant to stay in my life for a season.

Very shortly after Phil and I broke up, one day when Semona-Jane was driving my car, I got so fed up with her controlling my car that I told her I needed it. On that day, unlike on other days, I was very firm. I dropped her at the bus station in Seven Sisters. I just needed some alone time in my car. I wanted to feel as if my car belonged to me for a change. I was so fed up with being told what to do in my own car. This is when Semona-Jane met Jason.

Jason was tall – approximately six feet. He had a light complexion, and he was a handsome man. I loved Jason's spirit right from the start. He was just a very sweet man. Jason and Semona-Jane dated for two years, then Jason proposed to her. I could not have been happier for them both. However, this is when I found out just how little I really meant to Semona-Jane. I did everything for her. She still did not have a car at this stage. I took her wedding dress shopping, bridesmaids dress shopping, and would you believe it, she did not even ask me to be one of her bridesmaids! Ouch, ouch! That hurt so much. Even the caterer could see the bond we had. He thought I was her sister and wondered why I was not playing a part in the wedding. I had lost count of the number of people who asked the same question. One day the pressure got to me, and I broke down crying to Semona-Jane. I said to her, 'I thought we were sisters!' She very coldly said, 'You're not my sister!' I was heartbroken. I still continued to do everything for her right up until her wedding day. My last task on her wedding day was to provide her and her bridesmaids with breakfast. I was not even allowed in her house after making them breakfast! The wedding was absolutely beautiful! I was happy for them. I drove Semona-Jane and her husband to their honeymoon hotel, and after the weekend when they were on their way to their real honeymoon, I drove them to the airport and collected them from the airport on their return.

THE BREAK-UP

A SHORT TIME AFTER SEMONA-JANE'S WEDDING, I was still going through the process of my divorce. Phil made it as difficult as possible for me. He refused to sign the papers. He just would not do what was required of him. Phil even went and complained to my pastor. He told my pastor that he knew he would never find another woman like me, and no matter what he had to do, one day he would get me back! Again this was all talk.

It took me five years to get divorced from Phil!

Shortly before my divorce, Ethan began to have problems in school. He was only ten when Phil and I started divorce proceedings. If anyone had told me that Phil would behave like this towards his son, I would have said, 'No way!' Phil and Ethan were so close, and as soon as Phil and I broke up, Phil would not see his son. Ethan was devastated. He went from having his dad there every day, to not seeing him at all. I had to take action. I told Phil about the negative impact his decision was having on Ethan, but he just did not seem to care.

So one day I packed a bag for Ethan, and I decided to drop Ethan off on Phil's doorstep. I decided, if that woman wanted my husband, then let her see the damage she is doing to his son. I waited for her to open the door. I saw her take Ethan inside, then I drove off. Phil was not giving me any child support for Ethan either. My plan worked. I hated to put our child through this. I'm not proud of this, but Phil was soon on the phone to me negotiating time to spend with his son. We agreed that Phil would pick his son up on Wednesdays, as this was the day Phil did not work. I thought that Phil would spend some time with Ethan, as he was only seeing him once per week, but I guess that did not fit in with his new lifestyle. Phil would pick Ethan up, drive to McDonalds, which was two minutes away from our house, get him something to eat, and bring him straight back home. So out of a whole week, Phil would spend half an hour with his son. This was terrible. I tried to make Phil see that he was not hurting me, he was hurting our son, but nothing changed.

I never chased Phil for child maintenance. Ethan grew more and more despondent. I could see that he was not trying to be around his dad anymore. He was just angry at his dad. After seeing Ethan crave his father's attention, and then seeing Phil just keep on pushing Ethan away, I decided to get some counselling for Ethan. When there is a breakup of a marriage, and children are involved, no matter how you try to shield them, the children suffer too. I did not want this to have an adverse effect on our child, so I did the best thing I knew for Ethan.

The other two boys were much older, so they dealt with the divorce in their own way, but Ethan was only ten years old. When I took Ethan to the counsellor, certain things were revealed that really opened my eyes to Phil's behaviour in our marriage. Ethan was asked to express himself through drawing and so forth. One of the things Ethan drew was his daddy's van parked outside that woman's house, and Ethan was sitting in the living room of her house. Whilst he was sitting in the living room, he could see in a mirror in the hallway that his dad was kissing that woman. Ethan asked the counsellor, 'Why was my daddy kissing that woman like he kissed my mom?' Ethan also revealed that, whilst I was away in Atlanta at the T.D. Jakes conference, he and his daddy had slept at that woman's house. Phil had told Ethan not to tell me. How could Phil put this kind of pressure on our young son? Had I not had Ethan counselled, none of these things would have been revealed. My poor little Ethan was carrying an emotional load he should never have been carrying. This was significant, as Phil had told his family that he'd only started seeing this woman when it was clear that we were breaking up. He had not told them that she was the cause of our breakup.

Having known Phil's family for over twenty years, I was so disappointed that I was treated like a leper. Nobody in the family wanted to speak to me. Only the younger generation, who quite honestly did not care, just treated me exactly the same as before. I was their aunty, and no matter who came afterwards, they still regarded me as their aunty. That really made me feel good, because no matter what, when you love people, you just don't stop loving them because something happens. True love is not conditional.

During the time Phil and I were together, we had taken a family vacation every year. Our first vacation abroad was in 1986 when we went to America to visit my family and Phil's family as well. I had not seen my grandma since I was sixteen years old, and it was a blessing that, at the time we were visiting America, Grandma had come to visit Elizabeth. All my sisters and brothers were in America, and I had actually got to meet Zavier for the first time. You will remember that Zavier was my brother whom Elizabeth had given away. Elizabeth, Grandma, Hyacinth, Zavier, and Claudia met us at the airport. We were to stay with Elizabeth. For the first time in my life, Elizabeth hugged me at the airport. She actually lifted me off my feet. I was so taken aback by this. My mother had never hugged me before; she had never shown any affection to me before. *Elizabeth has certainly changed*, I thought. *If this is for real, I sure like it.*

It was on this trip that Elizabeth and my grandmother, Suzanna, took me into a room and closed the door behind them. All kinds of thoughts were racing through my mind. What were they going to tell me? I was a bit big for beatings, so, no, that could not be it. I hadn't done anything wrong that I knew about, so that couldn't be it either. Oh, Lord, what had I done? I was shaking with fear, but at least I knew that Phil was close by, so I could just scream for help if I needed to. Elizabeth and Suzanna told me that my father had not died when Elizabeth was five months pregnant with me, as Elizabeth had told me when I was growing up. The real story was that Suzanna would not allow my father to marry Elizabeth because he smoked marijuana at the time. This was a bad thing in those days. Suzanna did not want my father to have anything to do with me, so Suzanna and Elizabeth concocted the story to tell me that my father was dead. This is what I believed whilst I was growing up. So for thirty-six years of my life they lived a lie, and they allowed me to live a lie too. Here I was, at my age, being told, 'Your father didn't die after all. He may be alive and well somewhere in Jamaica.' They did not even have a picture to show me of what my father looked like. How was I supposed to digest this information? What was I to do with this information?

To this day, I have no idea what my father looks like. Every time I ask Elizabeth about my father, she is very tight lipped about the whole affair. I could barely get his name out of her. I am hoping that God will preserve my father's life so that one day I will be able to go to Jamaica and find him before he dies. My father does not even know what I look like. He never saw me as a little girl growing up; he was not allowed to see me. All I know is that my father is half Indian, and I know his name. That's all.

This was not the way I wanted to start my vacation, but at least now I knew the truth about my father. Whilst we were there, since Elizabeth seemed to be in a place in her life where I thought she would be able to deal with some information of my own, I decided that I would reveal the story of the rape. I discovered that, as a child, my instincts had been right. My mother did not believe me. She went and told my brothers and sisters that I was lying, that I had not been raped, because one day she put her hand on Mr Nash's crotch as he bent down, and she did not feel his penis, so he was a eunuch. I could not believe someone could be such a wicked liar. Why would I need to make up such a story? Elizabeth had not changed after all. I did not let this ruin our holiday!

Elizabeth had a very big house, which was cockroach infested. Phil and I found this out at the worst possible time. We were in bed, and as you know, when the lights are out, that's when the bugs come out to play. This was like something out of a horror movie. All of a sudden, I felt something fall on me. I screamed and jumped out of the bed only to hear and feel a crunch under my feet. To our absolute horror, we looked up to see roaches falling from the ceiling. The apartment on the floor above was roach infested, so at night, the bugs invaded my mother's apartment. There were so many of them. Needless to say we could not sleep. Phil and I sat up all night long fighting off cockroaches. The next day, we booked into a hotel for a few days, because we were due to visit Phil's aunt in another state, which was where we were to finish up our vacation.

Phil and I had purposely planned our vacation that way, because as you will remember, Elizabeth and I had not always got along, so we had decided it might be better to be safe than sorry. All said and done, the time we spent with Elizabeth and my family was nice except for the roach episode. We would meet up, and they would take us around, and we would do shopping and sightseeing, although we had to pay for the gas to do so.

Since 1986, every year we would go to America to see Elizabeth and the rest of my family, and every time we went, we would shop for my whole family, always bringing them gifts. Not once had Phil and I or our children gone to America and had come back with a single gift from my family. We did not allow this to affect our decision to shop for them; we still continued to shop for them every year we went. We would spend a small fortune; it would just have been nice if even once, one of my children had received a gift. It would have been nice if they could have said, 'My grandma bought this for me.' But this never happened.

THE BIG MOVE

When Phil and I broke up, I really wanted a change of scenery, and I believed that Ethan would also benefit from a change as well. I prayed long and hard, seeking the Lord for direction on this matter. I felt that I was being led to go to America, and besides, I did not know my family. When I left home, my youngest sister was only two years old. Now she was married with children of her own. There was a yearning inside of me for my family. I felt as if I was missing out on them. I would dream of the day when I would be able to go shopping with my sisters, and I yearned for the day when I could have a dinner party with my family. I longed to go to the beach with them, for example. I just wanted to do family stuff with my family. Ever since I was sent away at sixteen years old, everything I had done was with someone else's family. I wanted my own family. I wanted to get to know my family. I had missed out on so many years with them.

My family, on the other hand, have always been together; they have always had each other. I was the odd one out, along with my brother James. Hence, when Elizabeth invited Ethan and I over to stay with them in Florida, I jumped at the chance, because Elizabeth lived alone in a three-bedroom house. This was very convenient, because I would have my mother to show me the dos and don'ts until we got on our feet. At least that's what I thought. I also had my sister Hyacinth on the phone constantly. She was in the army, and she was always calling and encouraging me to come over. My sister Claudia was a regular caller as well, always asking, 'When are you coming to join us? We really miss you and can't wait for you to come over.'

After much deliberation, I decided that I would sell the house, and Ethan and I would go to America to live. Phil Junior had already left home, and he was doing quite well for himself working in the city of London as an accountant. Timothy had just finished university. They both had their own homes. Phil Junior had just given me my first granddaughter, Cherish. She was absolutely gorgeous. It was hard to leave my children behind, but they both had their own lives and were very independent. Because of the way in which I had seen Elizabeth treat her husband, one thing I made sure of was that all my boys were able to wash, cook, iron, and clean for themselves. They were pretty self-sufficient, so I knew that, whilst I was away, I would never have to worry about them not being able to take care of themselves.

I put the house up for sale, and everyone who came to view the house wanted to buy the property. But for some reason, even people who already had houses and wanted to buy our house for investment purposes were not able to do so. Their mortgages just would not come through. One by one they would fall through. None of these people was able to explain what was happening, and neither was I. I just did not understand what was going on. After several months of this, my young son Ethan said to me, 'Mom, why don't you ask Phil Junior if he would like to buy this house?' I had not thought about it, even though at the time Phil Junior was actively looking for a house to purchase. He was actually having the same problems. He would find a place, put a deposit down, and he would get gazumped at the last minute. He lost a lot of money in this process.

It would seem the Lord always used Ethan to tell me things, as I would discover later on. Ethan was so much wiser than his years. Six weeks before I was due to go away, I visited Phil Junior and asked him if he would consider buying my house. He jumped at the opportunity. Somehow, I just thought the house would be too big for him. It was a four-bedroom house with a garage, extended kitchen, two bathrooms, a patio, and lots of parking space.

Phil started looking into the mortgage, and to my surprise, within one month, the mortgage had come through. We completed on the house within thirty days. It gave me great joy just to walk away with one suitcase of clothes. I had given away the rest. I left everything for Phil Junior – china, bedding, furniture, garden furniture, crystal, you name it. I just simply walked away and left it. He moved in the day I was leaving for America with his fiancée and little Cherish.

Ethan and I jetted off to America and were met at the airport by Hyacinth and April. We got to America on the Thursday evening. Elizabeth did not know Ethan and I were coming; we wanted to surprise her. The plan was, we would stay at April's house the Thursday and Friday, and Ethan and I would show up at church on the Saturday. My family were Seventh Day Adventists. However, when we got to April's house, I had never in my entire life seen such a mess. April did not work and had two little girls, my nieces. They were beautiful. There were cockroaches everywhere. I actually witnessed the baby pick up a dead roach. She was about to put it in her mouth until I stopped her. She was one year old at the time. There were even roaches in the fridge and in the freezer. Even in the dishwasher. April's car was also roach infested. Whenever Ethan and I had to go in April's car, it was a total ordeal, because there were always roaches crawling around. At any given time they would just appear out of nowhere. It was very evident why April's car was roach infested. She would buy fast food and let my nieces eat it in the car. April would just simply leave all the mess that the children would make in the car. She did not believe in cleaning. She pretty much ate fast food, and everything she cooked came out of a packet.

Ethan and I simply could not wait to get out of there. So we decided to go to Elizabeth's house on the Friday evening and surprise her there instead. When we got to Elizabeth's house, she seemed really glad that Ethan and I were there. The whole family gathered around on the Saturday evening, but not for the reasons Ethan and I thought they were there. It would become very evident later on why they had wanted us to come over. As I mentioned before, April did not work, so she offered herself to take Ethan and I around so that we could buy the clothes and other stuff we needed for the Florida weather. I had to get Ethan registered for school, and I also had to kit him out with suitable clothes for school.

In Orlando it is vital to have a car. The bus service is very irregular, and because the weather is so hot, you do not want to be waiting for a bus in the heat for an hour or two. The bus service is not like it is in England, and there is no train or tube service. I started to notice little things with my family, but I just dismissed them. Soon, I was not able to dismiss them anymore as they were becoming habitual. For example, every time April took Ethan and I out shopping, she would take us to the places she wanted to go, and not where we wanted to go. I had to fill up April's car with gas every week, sometimes twice per week, depending on where she wanted to drive to. Not only that, but every day that we were out, I would have to buy April and her children meals. If we left before lunch, I would have to buy them breakfast. Then I would buy them lunch. And if we were still out at dinner time, I would have to buy them dinner as well. Never once did April offer to buy Ethan or I anything. Whilst at Elizabeth's house, I noticed that whenever I went food shopping, all my sisters and brothers would miraculously turn up at the house the same day. They would eat all the food I had just bought, even though I had expected it to last Ethan and I for the week, including his drinks for school.

I had just got there, I was not working, and I was trying to buy things to set up a home. Whenever Elizabeth would accompany me to the store to do grocery shopping, I would always give her money for herself. I would tell her, 'Mom, take this, just in case you see something that you need. You'll be able to buy it.' I would give her no less than $25 each time. Elizabeth would take the money, then she would proceed to load up my cart with various items, and I noticed it was all expensive items. And she would not just pick up one of each item; she would pick up two or three of each item. We would get to the checkout, and I would be waiting for Elizabeth to pay for the items she had put in the cart, but she would just stand there and she would not contribute one cent towards the bill, despite the fact that I had given her money to do so.

I soon figured out what was going on, and I intended to fix it. Their thought process was that, because we were from England, we were stupid. One day I went to the greengrocers with Elizabeth, and this time I decided to be smart and only pick up a hand basket. I was ready for her on this day. No sooner had I picked up the basket than

Elizabeth started loading it up. Again I gave her money. I told her that I was not able to carry a heavy basket, as I had problems with my shoulder, so it would be best if she got her own basket. What a surprise! All of a sudden, Elizabeth did not want the items that she had been loading in my basket anymore. She simply took them out and put them back on the shelves. Needless to say, she did not get a basket of her own. So every time we went shopping from then on, I adopted this method. I would pick up just a few items, and when I bought Ethan's drinks for the week, I would put them under his bed! I stopped doing a weekly shop. Ethan and I started eating out more often, and I would buy only the items I needed if I was cooking at home.

Elizabeth's mortgage was only $500 per month, and she told me that I would need to pay her $550 per month for Ethan and I to stay with her. I would also need to contribute to the bills and buy our food. Now, Elizabeth would eat all the food I bought, because I was not going to cook for Ethan and me, and not share with Elizabeth, so in effect we were also buying her food. I didn't mind. She was my mother, so I happily did it. What I could not tolerate was the fact that Ethan and I had no privacy. There were no locks on our doors, and my sisters and brothers would go into our bedrooms whenever they came over, and just help themselves to our stuff without asking!

Ethan and I decided we needed our own place. April said she would keep an eye out, and I was grateful. April called me about one month after we were there to say excitedly that a place had become available on her street just a few doors away from her. Ethan and I were so excited. I went to view the place, put my deposit down, and we moved in a week later. We stayed at Elizabeth's house exactly one month and ten days and paid her $1,100 in rent plus bills and food.

Ethan and I moved into a three-bedroom house of our own, and when we moved in, we had no furniture, but it felt like heaven just to have our own privacy once again and our own space. At this exact time, I also bought a car. It was a beautiful car – a blue Lexus RX 300 only a year old with 16,000 miles on the odometer. It was like a brand-new car. This was like a dream come true. God gave me this car. When I went to the Lexus dealer, I looked around the lot but

113

I did not see anything I liked. Either the interior wasn't right or the exterior wasn't right, or if I liked one it had too many miles on it and so forth. I was about ready to leave when the salesman said to me, 'We do have another car that just came in. It's upstairs, as it has not even been cleaned as yet.' I said, 'Okay, I'll take a look at it.' When I looked at the car, I just fell in love with it. Perfect. It looked silver because it was metallic, but it was actually baby blue with cream leather interior, and it was a special edition. It had the spoiler on the back. The windows were fully tinted all around, and it was fully loaded. What sealed the deal for me was that it only had 16,000 miles on the odometer, and had had only one owner. I could hardly believe my luck. I bought it there and then, of course providing the Carfax report came back okay.

I did not need to be pay April to drive me around anymore. I had my own car now, and nobody needed to be so involved in my business anymore. The first night Ethan and I moved into our new house, we went to the store and bought blow-up beds. It was hilarious. We had an empty house and two blow-up beds. No pots. No pans. Nothing but our toothbrushes and our suitcases. Now that I could drive and go where we wanted to go, as opposed to where April wanted to go, I could proceed to get the things I needed to get to furnish our house.

Whenever we were with April, I always felt restricted somehow, because if I looked at something she would make comments like, 'Why do you want to buy that? It's too much money.' I perceived that there was an element of jealousy there, so I would find myself leaving most of the things I wanted to get when I was with her. At least now I did not have that problem.

Our little house was so cute. The grass was well manicured every two weeks by the landlord. There were all kinds of tropical foods growing in the back garden. There was a mango tree, a banana tree, an orange tree, a hot pepper tree, called Scotch Bonnet a hot pepper used a lot in Caribbean dishes, and also pineapple. I was ecstatic. I loved every bit of it. I just couldn't even believe that I could just go into my back garden and pick an orange from the tree and also pick a banana. This felt so unreal to Ethan and I. We felt as if we were living a dream in paradise. I can think of nothing more beautiful in the world than waking up in the morning with the sun just shining through the windows, and the sky is so beautiful and so blue. It felt like heaven waking up in this environment. I felt as if moving to Florida was one of the best decisions I had made in my entire life.

The house itself was not big, but it was very compact. It had everything Ethan and I needed. My bedroom was en suite with a huge bathroom. It had a full bathtub and also a separate shower, which was very nice. Ethan had his own bathroom, which was also quite big, although it was not en suite. There was plenty of wardrobe space, and although I would have liked the kitchen to be a bit bigger, it was well maintained and had everything I needed.

My family were always trying to find out how much I sold my house in England for, and how much money I had, but I would never tell them, because I felt this was none of their business. I could see certain cracks appearing, and the facade that they had been putting up was fast unravelling. I would worship with my family on a Saturday, but really I hated it, and so did Ethan. I felt their worship was very hypocritical. For example, the ladies could not wear pants to church, but they wore pants during the week. If that's a normal part of your attire all week long, then why should you pretend that you don't wear it on a Saturday? The ladies were also not allowed to wear jewellery. What? That's just nonsense to me. As far as I am concerned, jewellery completes my outfit, and I cannot be so hypocritical to pretend that I don't wear or like jewellery. Again, I would see these people wearing jewellery during the week, but just not on Saturdays. That made no sense to me, and I just could not be a part of that. This is just my view, and one of my little pet peeves about this practice. I would see certain people in church on a Saturday looking holier than thou in a long, flowing skirt or dress, but then during the week, they would be wearing the tiniest shorts you can find!

I decided I wanted to worship on a Sunday as Ethan and I had done for years. Of course my family did not like it, but I had to be true to who we were. I was a grown woman, and I was not there to please my family. I've always been seen to be the black sheep of the family, so what was new? Nothing had changed. I would not conform; I had my own opinions. I had to do what felt right to me!

Soon afterwards, my sister Claudia started telling me about a thing called 'The Circle'. The Circle was meant to be a Christian group of ladies who got together to pray all around the world and share fellowship. During this process, each lady would put $5,000 on the table, which was called their gifting table. Their only obligation was to bring in two other ladies who would then bring in two other ladies, and each lady would contribute $5,000. When there were enough ladies on each table, the table would form a circle, and that's when the table would split and the next person in line would receive $40,000. Each lady who came on the table had to be invited on. When invited on to the table, that lady would have to be able to put down her gift of $5,000 to the table. This table had been in operation for over twenty years, and anyone from anywhere in the world could join so long as she was a Christian. There was a meeting each week that all the members of each table had to attend by way of a conference call. There were hundreds of tables all around the world.

When Claudia invited me to The Circle, I was very sceptical, and I said no way. However, she kept on insisting that I join, so I told her that, when she had received her money from the table, then I would consider it. Indeed, Claudia received her $40,000 and paid $5,000 so that Hyacinth would be able to come on the table as well. I was still not convinced. I knew that she had been gifted the $40,000, but I needed more information. Claudia got one of the organizers to give me a call, and I had a meeting with her. Juanita explained the whole concept of the table, showing me figures of how many ladies had been gifted all around the world, and she too had been gifted $40,000 on many occasions. I was invited to listen in on one of their conference calls, and I was impressed. This was actually real. I heard many women from all different nationalities from all walks of life expressing how this Circle had changed their lives. Claudia had also paid the $5,000 for Elizabeth to go on The Circle, and Elizabeth had also been gifted $40,000. The Circle moved quite quickly depending on how fast each lady would bring on her two ladies. If each lady brought on her two ladies immediately, then the gifting could take place within a few weeks.

Having witnessed my sister, my mother, and one of the organizers receive their $40,000, I decided to try to see if this was really the case, although I still felt unsure. I did not feel that I was taking any risk, because I was given a written guarantee that, if anything went wrong, my gift would simply be returned to me. So the worst thing that could happen, I thought, was that something could go wrong, but I would at least get my money back. I gifted the table and bought on my two ladies as requested. Very soon I received $40,000.

I was elated, so my sisters Angel and April asked me if I could lend them $5,000 each so they too could join The Circle. Of course they were my sisters, and I thought nothing of helping them to join. Many people who helped others onto The Circle requested a part of their $40,000, but I told my two sisters that all I wanted was just the $10,000 that I put down for them. They agreed to this, and I was fine with that. I decided to invest in this table because I wanted to buy a house of my own, and this was a good way to be able to make the purchase in mostly cash and have a small mortgage to pay. I also lent $15,000 to help three other people onto the table, and I gifted $5,000 for each of my three children. I also gifted $5,000 for my best friend Semona-Jane. I decided to invest $15,000 for myself. Semona-Jane's table was the first to come through, so I sent her $35,000. I was happy I could do that for her. Now it was the turn of the next tables to come through, but – shock and horror – all of a sudden, the tables collapsed.

Apparently a group of ladies from the Virgin Islands had invited their friends to The Circle and, through greed, they had decided to charge people to get onto the tables, and as a result these ladies decided to set up their own tables, which were bound to collapse, because there was a system to this table. These tables were based on prayers and fellowship with one another, and they broke that bond with greed. So the tables that had been helping women for years all of a sudden were no more, and worse, no one got any money back. This went to court, as several ladies were aggrieved at not getting their money back, as we all had it in writing that should anything go wrong, we would get our $5,000 back. I took a huge hit. I had invested money that should have helped my family and me, and here I was $60,000 out of pocket. I just had not seen this coming. I was not in a good place.

By this time, I had a job, so I was able to pay the rent and manage our day-to-day finances, but my savings had been wiped out. I felt so vulnerable. I thought all was not lost, because April had been gifted just before the table collapsed. I had lent her $5,000, so I waited for her to return that money. She lived just a few doors away from me, yet she did not tell me she had been gifted. I actually discovered this from the other ladies on that table. After waiting two weeks for April to pay me back the $5,000 I had lent her, I called her to enquire when I would receive the money. I told her I knew she had been gifted. I had noticed that, since April had been gifted, she had not been calling me, but I just thought she was busy. Yes, April had been very busy spending that money. She could not get me off the phone fast enough, and she did not show up to pay me any money either.

Christmas was fast approaching, and I had no money. Angel actually owed me $7,000, and my brother owed me $300. Surely one of them would pay me some of my money back. After all, when I lent it to them, they had been happy and in good spirits, so now that I was in need, they should be glad to help me out. I had helped them out when they were in need, right? And they were my family, right? Besides, I was not asking for a loan. The money they owed me was mine! I was just asking for it back, as I really was in need of it.

Well, to date, April has paid me back $200 out of $5,000, and remember she got gifted $40,000, which she would never have gotten unless I had lent her that $5,000. April used the money right under my nose to buy a new dishwasher, new washing machine, and new dryer. She bought her children complete new wardrobes along with many other things. I was right there, just a few doors away, with nothing. I could not even afford to buy my son Ethan a Christmas present, and she would not give me back the money I had loaned her, even though she had it to give back to me.

Angel did not get gifted, but I told her I needed the $2,000 she had for me. To date, I have never asked Angel for that $5,000, and she has never mentioned it. Angel gave me $100 at Christmas from the $2,000 she owed me. My bills were due – everything. Angel's Christmas tree was piled high with gifts for her children, and she would not give me the money that I loaned her. I did not even bother to ask my brother, because he was not working, and I knew he did not have any money to give me. This was the first time I experienced just how selfish and mean my family really were. I suddenly thought of Semona-Jane! Surely she's my best friend. She will help me out. When I told Semona-Jane the situation I was in, she never even offered to lend or give me a dime. What a friend!

MY DEAR FRIEND, JULIANNA

I HAD MET THE MOST AWESOME people through The Circle, and to this day we are still in touch with each other. One of the ladies that I met was Rosie, and I was introduced to her entire family. Rosie lived in New Jersey at the time. She had two sons and one daughter, Julianna. Julianna had one daughter, Sasha. I so loved Julianna. Whenever I called to speak to Rosie and Julianna answered the phone, we would talk for ages, so much so that sometimes we would forget that I had initially called to speak with Rosie.

Julianna had a disease called lupus, and sometimes she would get very ill. It was at these times in particular that Julianna and I would talk the most. I would encourage her, and just let her know that God would never give her more than she could bear. One night, Julianna called, and she told me the doctors wanted her to go into the hospital, as they needed to run some tests on her. Julianna and I were laughing and joking. She told me she needed to rest for a few days. She was in great spirits. We talked several times whilst she was in the hospital. Rosie did not like the hospital, and at first she did not want to go and see her daughter.

Julianna was only meant to be in the hospital for a few days, but the tests that they were conducting were not going very well. I got a call from Julianna, which had me worried. She was the most positive person I knew, so when she started telling me that she was just so tired, and she could not take anymore, I was alarmed. We spent about an hour talking on the phone. I encouraged her and prayed with her. By this time, Rosie had made it to the hospital and spent most days with her daughter. The very next day I got a call from Rosie. She was crying, and in pieces. I felt so helpless. They were in New Jersey, and I was in Orlando, and because of my immigration status at the time, I was unable to travel. Rosie informed me that Julianna was in intensive care, and she was in a coma on a life-support machine.

I mustered up every bit of energy I had to encourage Rosie. Inside of me, I was broken in pieces, but I had to be strong for my friend. I waited anxiously over the next forty-eight hours encouraging Rosie along the way through my own pain. Rosie called me again. This time she was not crying; she seemed rather calm, and I thought that she was going to tell me Julianna was fine, but I could hardly believe the words that were coming from her mouth. Rosie told me that they had made the decision to switch off the life support machine, and Julianna had gone home to be with the Lord. At first, I thought this was a cruel joke, and then I said, 'What did you say?' I had heard her the first time, but was just unable to grasp what I had heard. I was numb with pain, and I just burst out crying. I could no longer contain myself.

How could Julianna be gone from us? She had been so beautiful, and so full of life. How was this possible? Had I known when I had last spoken to Julianna, that it would be our last conversation ever, I would have told her so much more. I would have told her just how much I loved her, and just how much she meant to me. But I did not get the chance to tell her; so much was left unsaid. Deep down, the only thing that gave me comfort was that I believed that Julianna knew that I really loved and cared for her. I got off the phone, and I wept from my very being. I cried so hard. Everything that was in me was in pieces.

I was with a friend at the time I received this news, and I only realized how much my crying was affecting him when he also started crying, and he had never met Julianna. This stopped me dead in my tracks. I said, 'Why are you crying?'

Rosie and I were the type of friends that knew how to be naked with one another. We cried together; we laughed together. In the months that lay ahead of us, our friendship would be tested to the maximum. Julianna was only thirty-nine years old when she died. She was Rosie's only daughter. In the coming months, Rosie moved to Orlando, as all her family were there, and she needed all the support she could get. We spent a lot of time together. There was a time when I wondered if Rosie was going to make it. She grieved for her daughter so long and so hard. All I could do at times was just to be there for her. We would be in the supermarket, and Rosie would just burst out crying. It was the simple little things sometimes that would remind Rosie of Julianna. I cannot say that I knew how Rosie felt, but I sure empathized with her pain. She was experiencing the pain that only a mother who has lost a child can relate to.

Julianna was one of God's beautiful angels who was here on earth with us for a short period of time, and I am truly blessed to have known such a beautiful person. She was truly an inspiration to me, as throughout her illness, she never once complained. Julianna was a tribute to Rosie and her family. During her short time on this earth, Julianna had accomplished so much. She had done more with her life than most people accomplish in a whole lifetime.

THE FIRE

I TOLD ROSIE ABOUT MY SITUATION at Christmastime, and how my family would not help me. I only knew Rosie from praying and fellowshipping on the table. We had never met face to face at that time, but she sent me a $500 gift. I was able to pay some bills and buy my son Ethan a Christmas present. A total stranger saved our Christmas, and my entire family was right there, but did not care to help. All they cared about was just themselves.

Christmas came and went, and we were now well into the New Year. It was now June, exactly a year since I had moved into our house. The landlord informed me that he was selling the house, as he needed to put his daughter through college. He asked me if I wanted to purchase the house, but although I liked the house, I just needed more space. I decided to look for a property to buy. I was paying so much money in rent each month, and I could use this money to pay a mortgage instead. I did not know many people in Orlando, so I asked Rosie if she knew a good real estate agent whom I could use to purchase a house. It so happened that her son was an agent. Wow! And he actually lived not too far away from where I was living. I got Sean's details from his mother, and I got in touch with him.

Sean arranged for Ethan and me to see some properties. We fell in love with one property immediately. It was a two-bedroom house, but it was much bigger than the three-bedroom that we were living in. It had a huge patio and good-size back and front gardens The bedrooms were absolutely huge. It was on two floors, which Ethan and I really liked. It kind of reminded us of home! There was one bedroom downstairs, which was en suite, and there was a huge hallway followed by a large living room and dining room. The kitchen was not overly big, but it was a fair size as well. It was well equipped with everything I needed. There was also a garage. I liked this house a lot. There was also a bedroom upstairs, which, again, was en suite, and this bedroom was absolutely huge. It had a lot of character in that it was L shaped. The hallway was so huge, you could actually fit another bedroom in it.

I told Sean that I really liked that house, and he put the wheels in motion to see if I could get a mortgage. Now, because I had been in the country only for a year, I had not yet established a credit history. I had bought my car outright. I had bought all our furniture outright, so I didn't owe anyone anything. I was debt free. Sean asked if I knew anyone who would be willing to put the mortgage in his or her name for about six months, after which time I could change it over by doing a quitclaim deed. This would enable me to get the mortgage at a decent interest rate. Because I was a foreigner, the interest rates for me would be astronomical.

Most evenings while I was driving home from work, I would speak to Elizabeth on the phone, and this particular evening I mentioned to Elizabeth what Sean had told me about the mortgage. I knew that Elizabeth had been in the United States for over twenty years, and I figured that she would know someone trustworthy whom she could recommend who might be willing to put the mortgage in his or her name for me temporarily. To my surprise, Elizabeth said that she would do it. I was truly shocked, and I actually felt quite close to her, just thinking that she would do that for me. I asked her if she was sure, and she said absolutely, but there was only one thing she would ask of me. I enquired as to what that might be. She told me not to tell any of my brothers and sisters that she was doing this for me. I readily agreed, because as I said earlier, I am a private person, and I hated the fact that everyone seemed to know my business.

I called Sean to let him know that my mother said that she would take out the mortgage for me in her name. Although I was excited that Elizabeth was doing this for me, I did not want her to feel pressured, or feel that she was getting into anything that she did not understand. I wanted to ensure that Elizabeth knew exactly what she was offering to do. I asked Sean to visit her at home and sit and explain everything to her. That way, if she had any questions, she could ask them of him. He visited her at home, and they made arrangements to proceed. I was not present at this meeting. Elizabeth seemed quite happy, and she seemed to like Sean. She commented what a lovely young man he was, and how he had taken the time to explain everything to her, and answered all of her questions. I was happy to hear this. I was really not much involved in the process except to pay money when required, as I did not know anything about the house-buying system in America.

The offer I made on the house was accepted, and the time came when the papers needed to be signed. I was not even there for the signing of the papers. I just trusted Elizabeth to take care of that. She did not require me to be there, so I went to work. When the signing was completed, Sean called to say that everything was done. I was ecstatic. I now had a house. Just a few more bits and pieces to do, then I would be able to move into my very own house in Florida. It sure felt good.

When it came time to actually move into our new house, money was scarce, as I had just about spent everything I had to complete the purchase of the house. Ethan and I were happy; we pretty much had everything we needed. We moved into our new home, and within a week we had unpacked everything. We did not want to prolong the process, and besides, I had so many ideas about what I wanted to do to our new home. So, to be honest, the sooner things got unpacked, the sooner I could start.

On the first weekend we were going to spend in our new home, I invited Elizabeth over for dinner. It was the first meal I was preparing in our new home, so it was really special. Once we had moved in, I had noticed that there was a leak in the kitchen, and it seemed to be coming from my bathroom upstairs. I called my brother Luke, who is a plumber, and when he looked at the leak, he said he knew exactly what it was. He told me that the pipe in my bathroom had become worn and rusty, so he just needed to cut that piece of pipe out and replace it with a new piece. No problem, I thought, simple enough to fix, so I gave him the money to buy the pipe, and I promised to pay him for doing the job. Luke wanted to do the job immediately, and that worked for me, as I needed to stop the leak. This was on the Sunday that Elizabeth was coming over for dinner.

I was busy cleaning up and cooking dinner at the same time. Luke was busy in my bathroom installing the new piece of pipe after cutting the bad piece out. All of a sudden, I saw smoke in the kitchen, and bits of the insulation from the pipes in my bathroom began to fall through the ceiling from upstairs. They were on fire! I called up the stairs and asked Luke if everything should be smoking up like that, and he said, 'This is what I do for a job! I know what I am doing. You have nothing to worry about.' So I carried on doing what I was doing.

I was getting a bit bothered, because the smoke was now filling up the whole house, and again I asked Luke if everything was okay. He yelled at me this time, saying, 'I told you everything is fine!' I said, 'Okay.'

As Ethan had been an asthmatic as a baby, I took him outside into the patio, because I did not want the smoke to trigger an asthma attack. We were both standing in the patio when I saw Luke run outside. He was now wearing a mask. I was getting worried. I followed him inside. Next thing I saw was Luke running upstairs with buckets of water. He was still telling me everything was fine, and he had it under control.

All of a sudden, I heard banging at my front door. I was a bit shocked. Why did my visitor not just ring the doorbell? I opened the door. It was my next-door neighbour, Jim. 'Semone, your house is on fire!' he shouted. I said, 'It's okay, but thank you. Everything is under control.' I went back inside.

No sooner had I gone back inside, than I heard banging on my door again. I went to the door again, only this time to see my other neighbour, Wendy. 'Semone, your house is on fire!' I told her the same thing – everything was fine – and I went back inside.

The smoke was thick in the house at this stage, but my brother was still telling me everything was fine. He was still telling me not to worry. Next I heard more banging on my front door, and the doorbell was ringing at the same time. I opened the door to the fire brigade, and I saw six fire engines outside my house! 'Ma'am,' said one of the fire fighters, 'I need you to get out of the house immediately!' I said, not realizing the seriousness of the situation, 'Can I just get dressed first?' At the time, all I had on was my nightdress. I still did not understand what all the fuss was about. And who had called them anyway? 'No,' he said, 'I need you out right *now*!'

So they led me out of the house along with Ethan and Luke. When I got outside, pretty much everyone who lived on the street had assembled outside my house. What I had not been able to see from inside was that smoke was billowing out from my bathroom window upstairs, along with angry-looking orange flames. Now I understood why my neighbours were telling me my house was on *fire!* The fire fighters cut a big hole in the side of my house, and they poked holes in the roof to ensure the insulation was not smouldering away, as this could reignite the fire.

Just then, the newspaper crew came along. I said to Ethan, 'You need to hide me! I am not going on national television looking like a victim! I am no one's victim!' I sat on a low wall around the front garden next door, and Ethan, with his six-foot-five-inch frame, stood in front of me. Then, just to make matters worse, it started to rain. God has a funny sense of humour.

At this stage, I just started crying. How could this be happening? I had only just moved into our new home! I'd been there for just one week! I sat on that wall and watched my dream go up in flames. This was heartbreaking. The fire fighters reported that lightning had hit the house. For insurance purposes, I went along with that report, and Luke readily agreed, but Luke knew he had caused that fire, and no lightning was involved.

The whole house was just a mess. The carpet was waterlogged. Everything was smoke damaged. It was just as well I had gotten insurance. Ironically, Sean had insisted that I get insurance; I had actually wanted to postpone getting it, because I had no money at the time. Sean actually put up his own money to make sure I had insurance. Look at God work!

The fire fighters asked if I had somewhere to stay, as they could have provided accommodation through various charities such as the Red Cross. Before I could respond, my other brother, Roger, arrived and said, 'Yes, she has plenty of places to stay. Our mother has a three-bedroom house.' I was not happy. I just wished he would shut up. The last place I wanted to be going back to was Elizabeth's house. I now had no choice, so I packed up our valuables and two TVs, one for my room and one for Ethan's room. As I figured the repairs on the house would not take long, I agreed to stay at Elizabeth's. I thought the repairs would not take more than a month. With Ethan in school and me at work, we figured we could just about manage that.

The cleanup process on the house was exhausting. The insurance I had was pretty good. The very next day the company sent someone around to take away everything in the house for cleaning. They took all my clothes and Ethan's, all our shoes, my handbags, towels, curtains, bedding – just about everything, which was a blessing. They had a field day with my stuff, however, because when I got them back, some were damaged and some had gone missing. That part was just a nightmare.

THE DECEPTION

THERE JUST NEVER SEEMS TO be a time when there is no drama in my life!

One Sunday, after Ethan and I had been staying at Elizabeth's house for two weeks, I drove Ethan to football practice at his school. I planned to run a few errands before going back to pick him up. Whilst I was out running my errands, I got a call from the real estate agent, Sean. To my utter disgust, Sean said the most chilling words to me: 'Semone, they want your house!' I stammered, 'Wha—what are you talking about?' I could hardly get my words out.

Sean started to explain himself: 'Some dude calling himself Roger – said he's your brother – called me and started swearing at me. He said I forced his mom to sign papers for your house! He wants me to sign your house over to him and his sister Hyacinth!' Sean was so distraught. He said, 'Semone, why did you not tell me your family was like that? I could have protected you!' I said, 'How so?' Sean said, 'I could have had Elizabeth co-sign for you so that your name would be on the house.' No one could ever have imagined a mother behaving in that manner. None of my sisters or brothers had said a word to me. All of this had been going on behind my back. Every day Elizabeth would kiss Ethan and me goodbye when we left the house, and every evening she would be as nice as pie. I was just dumbfounded.

I was shocked to the core! Only then did I realize that I was dealing with a dangerous set of people. They were smiling in my face, but behind my back they were turning the knife. Ethan and I were not safe at Elizabeth's house. We could not spend another night there! I went back to pick up Ethan and told him what was happening. Although we had nowhere else to go, I knew we could no longer stay at Elizabeth's. There was not even water in our house, but at least the carpets and walls were now dry, because the insurance company had sent in a company to remove the water and ventilate the house.

Ethan and I decided that we would not say anything to Elizabeth. We did not want to alert her to the fact that we knew what she was up to. I knew that, if Elizabeth knew that Ethan and I knew what she was up to, then she would try to hold our stuff captive. We decided that we would go to Elizabeth's and behave as normal, but then we would very quietly load our stuff into my car – the most expensive stuff first. Elizabeth was relaxing in the family room, which was at the back of the house, so did not realize what we were doing. We actually completely loaded up the car with most of our stuff before she realized.

I drove to our house, which was no more than a ten-minute drive from Elizabeth's house, and we unloaded our stuff. We had been gone from Elizabeth's house for only forty-five minutes or less. Believe it or not, by time we got back to her house, she'd had someone come in to change the lock on her front door. I could not believe it. I rang the doorbell, and eventually she let us in, and we got the rest of our stuff, only because she did not want what was left. We had already taken all the good stuff. Once we finished loading up, Ethan and I went to Elizabeth and thanked her for having us there. She did not even acknowledge us, but as we were about to walk away, she said to me, 'Give me the keys to my house.' Wow! So that's what she was up to all along! I said, 'It is not your house, *Mom*. It's *my* house.' She snapped back, 'It's in my name. It's my house. Give me the keys.' I then pleaded to any form of decency she had inside of her. I said, 'Mom, please, don't do this, because if you do, you won't see me, Ethan, or any of your grandchildren again.' She looked up at Ethan, and then at me, and very cold-heartedly said, 'I don't care.' Those words ripped through our hearts. Ethan was heartbroken to hear, at fifteen years old, that his grandmother did not care if she ever saw him again. Ethan was just getting to know Elizabeth as his grandma, and she had just taken that away from him. I then said to her, 'Okay.

Come to the house and get the keys, because you will not be getting them from me.' With that said, I left and went back to our house.

I started getting threatening phone calls from Hyacinth and also from April. Every day I would get disgusting text messages, as I refused to answer the phone to acknowledge their barrage of insults. One such text was from April, who told me she was going to send me back to England in a body bag. My children were incensed. In one of Hyacinth's texts she wrote, 'How dare you? Who do you think you are? We've been here for years, and we don't have a house, so who do you think you are? You just got here and bought a house.' She further went on to say, 'Your house is horrible. It's just a stack of sticks. It's not even what I would call a house.'

I thought that I was so much better than they were! I was so shocked. These were the people to whom I had lent and given money. These are the people that I moved halfway across the world to be close to, to get to know as my family. I had bought them and their children clothes and all sorts of stuff for years. Wow, way to let your sister know how you really feel about her! The truth was coming out now. This was all happening because Elizabeth lied and told my brothers and sisters that I had forced her into signing for my house. I had not even been there when Elizabeth signed the papers! I now believe that, all along, Elizabeth had had a hidden agenda, and that is why she asked me not to tell my sisters and brothers she was doing that for me.

Phil Junior called Elizabeth hoping to talk some sense into her, but she became abusive to him on the phone and started cursing me. Only then did Phil Junior repeat to Elizabeth the same threat —exactly what April and Hyacinth had said they would do to me. He told her that he would do it to her, because I was his mother, and he was not going to sit back and allow anyone to disrespect me in that way. Oh my goodness, did they make a big deal out of that! Hypocrites! It was okay when they were threatening me, but when the shoe was on the other foot, they could not handle it.

What really amazed me was that none of my brothers and sisters came to me and asked me what had happened, with the exception of Zavier. Elizabeth treated my brothers and sisters as if they were precious treasures. She treated me as if I was dirt underneath her feet. Had it not been for Phil and me, *none* of my family would be in America. Had I not allowed Elizabeth to come to England and stay with Phil and me, had we not paid her fares and given her money to get to America, she would not have been able to get sponsorship from her employer, and get my brothers and sisters to America. How convenient that Elizabeth had not mentioned any of this to my brothers and sisters. What Elizabeth did tell them was that I allowed her to sleep on the floor when she came to England to stay with me, because I had brand new sofas at the time. What a wicked lie.

Why does my mother hate me so much that she would poison my brothers and sisters minds against me? What have I ever done to her? For my whole life, all I ever did was help Elizabeth, give and give and give to her! Why does she hate me? I remember speaking to Elizabeth about a will. I was alarmed to know that, at age sixty-six, she had not yet made a will. I was telling her that I had already made my will. Having worked for lawyers, I had seen what happens when someone dies without a will, and I was explaining this process to her. Lo and behold, Elizabeth went and told my sisters and brothers that I was trying to kill her off so I could get her belongings. Elizabeth had nothing that I wanted or needed.

Whenever I spoke to Elizabeth about anything, her response to me would be, 'I have to discuss it with my children.' I said to her one day, 'Am I not one of your children? Who am I?' She never responded. I know just how Joseph felt in the Bible, because my brothers and sisters hate me, and I have never done anything wrong to them. But with Elizabeth poisoning their minds, it's easy to see why they would hate me. At the same time, they are grown, they are adults, and they should be able to say, 'Semone has never done anything but render kindness to us.' On that basis alone they should be able to make an informed decision, but they seem to prefer to allow themselves to be poisoned by Elizabeth.

I know the day will come when Elizabeth will have to answer to God for her actions. My prayer for her is that, before she leaves this earth, she will ask God's forgiveness for the way that she treated my children and me.

132

THE AMBUSH

THE LONG CLEAN-UP PROCESS BEGAN on the house. Ethan and I had no water, because the house had been condemned as unfit to live in, so the fire fighters had turned off the water on the day of the fire. Ethan and I went to the store. I bought two big bowls and lots of bottled water. These we used for washing ourselves in our bathrooms. This went on for about two weeks. One day Jim, my next-door neighbour, knocked on my door. 'Semone,' he said, 'you do know you can turn the water back on, right?' I said, 'No, I had no idea. How do you do that?' Jim said, 'Follow me.' I followed him to the end of my front garden, and Jim turned the water back on for me. I was so grateful to have running water in the house. I don't know how Jim knew that we did not have any water, but he certainly was a great help.

Another two weeks went by, and two cheques came from the insurance company. They were meant to cover the repairs that needed to be made to the house. The only problem was that, because the house was in Elizabeth's name, the cheques also came in Elizabeth's name. I called my brother Luke, because we still had a good relationship despite the fact that he had caused the fire in my house. I held no malice against him. I looked at it for what it was, an accident pure and simple. I don't believe he did it on purpose. Luke was the only person I confided in that I had the cheques. I told him that I had planned to go and see Elizabeth to have her cut me a cheque in my name so I could get the repairs done on my house. The word of God says, 'The love of money is the root of all evil' (1 Timothy 6:10 King James Version).

Before I went to Elizabeth's house, I bought her a peace lily, because I was so fed up with all the fighting that was going on in the family. When I arrived, the first thing I noticed was Elizabeth's car sitting in the driveway. Now I found this very strange, because even if Elizabeth planned to go back out, she never left her car in the driveway. It was always in her garage. This kind of threw me a bit, but I just dismissed it. When I rang the doorbell, Elizabeth asked, 'Who is it?' I knew she knew it was I, because she could clearly see me through the net curtains. Also, my car was parked in full view of her window. I played the game, however, and said, 'It's Semone.' In a really mean and aggressive tone, she answered 'Whe yu want?' (What do you want?) I said, 'I have bought you a peace lily, Mom.' She answered, 'Put e dung de.' (Put it down there.) I said, 'I need to see you, Mom.' Again she asked 'Whe yu want?' So I said, 'Mom, I have the cheques, and I need to speak to you please.'

Quick as a flash, the door opened. I handed her the peace lily. She said, 'Put e dung de.' I said, 'Mom, why are you behaving like this?' No answer. She beckoned me to the family room, and we both sat down. I showed her the cheques and asked her to cut me a cheque so that I could deposit it in my account to get the work started on the house. Elizabeth took the two cheques and said she was going into her bedroom to get her chequebook. I noticed she closed the door behind her. She returned from her bedroom empty handed. I said, 'Mom, where is the chequebook?' She looked at me with a smirk on her face and said, 'I ain't giving you nothing.' I said, 'Mom, those cheques do not belong to you, and I need to get the work done on the house.' She reiterated, 'I ain't giving you nothing.' I said, 'Mom, God does not like ugly, and you know those cheques do not belong to you, but if that's how you feel, keep them.' I got up from the sofa and started heading for the door to leave. All of a sudden, her bedroom door opened, and out stepped my brother Roger, the one who had called Sean to have my house signed over to him and my sister Hyacinth. Roger is six foot five inches tall, I am only five four. I guess he was there to intimidate me. I tried telling him to speak some sense into Mom, but of course they were both in on it along with my other brother, Luke. I knew Luke had set me up, because as I said earlier, he was the only one I had told that I had received the cheques and was going to see mom.

THE COVER-UP

I THOUGHT THIS WAS BAD, BUT the worse was yet to come. I went back home totally despondent. My cell phone, along with Ethan's, was on the same plan as Elizabeth's. All of a sudden, I tried to use my phone, and I was unable to make or receive any calls. Elizabeth had reported our phones stolen, and the company had disconnected them. Elizabeth did this just to be spiteful, despite the fact that I had paid my bill faithfully every month.

There was a big hole in the side of my house. It was now coming up to the hurricane season in Florida, and there were also multiple holes in my roof. How could I live here under these conditions? I called home to speak to my children, Phil Junior and Timothy, to let them know what was going on. Phil Junior immediately jumped on a plane and came over to give me some moral support. The day Phil Junior came, we were all at home. Due to the lack of kitchen facilities, we decided to go and get something to eat. As we left our road, Ethan said to me, 'Mom, there's Grandma's car.' As I looked, I saw Elizabeth and my sister Claudia sitting in the car. I had an uneasy feeling that they were up to something. Why would they be sitting there just one street away from my house? So, I drove back home and left Ethan at home with strict instructions not to open the door, as he was a minor, and no one could force his or her way into the house without an adult being there. Ethan was now fifteen years old.

As Phil Junior and I left again to go to the shop to get some food, we saw Elizabeth once more. This time she was out of her car. There were also two police cars and three police officers with her and my sister. I could hear Elizabeth yelling, 'There she is! There she is!' She was pointing at my car when they saw me approaching. The police officer stepped into the middle of the road and signalled for me to stop by shining a light in circular motion directly at my car. I stopped the car in the middle of the road in front of the officer. I asked the officer if I could remove my car from the middle of the road so as not to restrict traffic, and she said yes, so I moved my car to the side of the road.

At this time my heart was pounding so loud, it felt as if it was about to jump right out of my chest. All the while, I was wondering what I had done to be stopped like this. I felt like a criminal. When I got out of the car, the officers told me that they had a summons for me to attend court. They were also there to escort me out of my home. I explained to them that the house was my house, but, whilst they empathized with me, they still had to enforce the order. When I read the order, I learned that Elizabeth had gone to court and taken out a summons against me. She claimed that I had committed domestic violence against her, and she had also taken out a restraining order against me. This was the reason she had parked one street away from my house, because she was not allowed to have contact with me either. I was shell-shocked. At no time in my life had I ever – neither would I ever – lift my hands to my mother! And even worse, when she saw Phil Junior, whom she had not seen for fifteen years, she told the officers that he had also committed domestic violence against her. He had only just got into the country that very day and had not had any contact with her! Was she insane?

Elizabeth and my sister Claudia left, and I was still speaking to the officers. I said to them, 'Look, I don't want to be escorted into my home by police officers. I haven't done anything wrong.' The officers could see that I was just not a violent person. They could see I would not hurt a fly, so one of them said to me, 'If we allow you to go back into the house, can you promise us that you will just pack a bag and leave as you've been requested to do?' I promised the officers that I would just go to the house and pack a bag, collect my son, and leave.

Suddenly Phil Junior and I no longer had an appetite. We were no longer hungry. I turned the car around and went home. I packed a bag as I had promised the officers, and we picked up Ethan. Phil Junior did not have to pack, because he had not yet unpacked. Here I was in a strange country. I was homeless, and I knew nobody whom

I could call on for help except for my friend Rosie, but Rosie was all the way in New Jersey; that would not help me now.

I drove around to see if I could find a decent, cheap hotel, and I finally found something in my budget. I put the two boys in one room, and I had a room of my own. I did not even get undressed. I just lay across the bed, my head spinning from the day's events. How could this be happening? Why was this happening to me? As long as the night was, I could not sleep. I had managed to get mobile phones for myself and Ethan after paying a large deposit – again, because I had no credit history. But at least now I had peace, because neither Elizabeth nor my sisters and brothers knew our new numbers, so I would not be getting those disgusting messages.

I had never in my whole life felt this kind of emotion. I felt as if I had let myself, and my children down. Here we were in a hotel with nowhere to live. Ethan and I were homeless! For the first time in my life, I knew how it felt to feel hopeless and helpless, all at the same time. It's a very thin line between sanity and insanity, because but for the grace of God that kept me, I would certainly have lost my mind, especially to know that I was suffering these things at the hands of my own mother!

The word of God says, 'My grace is sufficient for you, for my power is made perfect in weakness' (2 Corinthians 12:9 New International Version). I am living proof of this. Whilst lying on the bed, I kept hearing a voice in my head telling me to call Zavier. I heard the voice over and over again. Finally, I mustered up the strength and called him at around three in the morning. Zavier worked at night, so I knew he would be awake. He said, 'Semone, where are you? What happened to you? I have been trying to call you, but I could not get through.' Zavier said he had heard what they said, meaning my family, but he wanted to hear my side of the story. I told him exactly what had happened. He said, 'Semone, I believe you, because I have had similar dealings with Elizabeth.'

He made me know that I was not going crazy. Somehow I had felt as if I was just in a horrible nightmare, and I was going to wake up, and everything was going to be all right. Zavier revealed to me that, when Elizabeth was in the process of selling her house in New Jersey to move to Florida, she had borrowed a large sum of money from him. Zavier lent Elizabeth the money on the basis that he would be given the money back as soon as she had completed on her house. When Zavier asked Elizabeth for the money, her response was, 'What money?' And to this day, she has never paid him back. Zavier said, 'Okay, Semone, I'm going to ask you some questions about your property that only a homeowner would know the answer to.' At this stage, unknown to me, Elizabeth was going around telling everyone that my house belonged to her! I said, 'Okay.' Zavier asked me how much I had paid for the insurance on the house, and a few other questions. He then said, 'Semone, I'm going to call Mom and ask her these same questions I just asked you. If she is unable to answer them, then I will know who the house belongs to!' Zavier called Elizabeth, and she was unable to answer any of the questions. She knew that Zavier knew it was not her house, so she turned on the waterworks and just broke down crying, but Zavier was having none of it and told Elizabeth, 'Give Semone back her house!' He also told Elizabeth to give me back the money so I could fix up my house.

Elizabeth called me. She was crying on the phone and saying how sorry she was and that she had allowed the devil to come between us. Elizabeth also told me that she could not give me back all the money, because my brother Roger, my sister Hyacinth, and my other brother Luke had already split up the money between them. They had deposited it in their different accounts and had already used up some of it! Elizabeth had already arranged with Luke to do the work on the house and had given him some money to do so. However, I did not want Luke to do the work because of his previous track record. What would he set on fire this time? He was supposed to be a plumber, and if he made such a mess of just a small plumbing job, it stands to reason that he was not a builder. How was he going to be able to do an effective job on my house? Roger's response was that he would hire a friend who was a registered builder to do the work, and he would assist him. I did not believe this story. Zavier had also told Elizabeth to cancel the court hearing, because he did not want to see his mom and his sister in court fighting against each other. When Zavier questioned Elizabeth and asked her why she had told the court that I had committed domestic violence against her, Elizabeth told Zavier that those charges were the only thing she could think of at the time!

Ethan and I moved back into our house. We believed that Elizabeth had called the court and had cancelled the hearing, and everything was now fine, as she had told Zavier. She invited Ethan and I over to dinner, but there was just something inside of me that could not trust her. I just had a feeling. I could not quite put my finger on it, but something was telling me that something was not right. There were a lot of thoughts running through my head. Would she do something to my food? Was she setting me up for something else? I just could not shake these feelings.

Ethan did not want to go either, but my brother Roger kept on calling and insisting that we come. He even drove to my house to pick us up. I made an excuse, so Ethan went, but I did not want to go. As the evening was coming to a close, and Elizabeth kept on calling, Ethan called me and asked me to come. I decided to go, but I was still very reluctant. I could not bring myself to eat any of the food. I just pushed it around the plate. Elizabeth was crying those big crocodile tears, but it all seemed fake to me. I just felt numb around her. I felt very shaky around her. I somehow just could not easily forget the wickedness that she had been showing. I simply could not trust her anymore.

Weeks went by, and as the court date drew near, even though I believed that Elizabeth had cancelled the court hearing, I did not hear a word from Elizabeth. All of a sudden she just stopped calling. This aroused my suspicions even more. I knew something was not right. The day before the hearing was due to take place, I heard that voice again inside my head. This voice just kept on talking to me all day long. All I could hear was, 'Call the court. Call the court. Call the court.' It was literally like an alarm going off in my head, and it would not stop. So at around two in the afternoon, I just could not deal with hearing that voice anymore. I picked up the phone and called the court. I spoke to the clerk, and she informed me that the hearing was still scheduled for the next day. It had not been cancelled. She also stressed that, if I did not show up for the hearing, a warrant would be issued for my arrest.

I could not quite take all of this in. I was in total denial. I told myself that this was all a big mistake. It had to be, because Elizabeth had told Zavier that she had cancelled the hearing. Surely this clerk must have made a big mistake. I waited for around a half an hour, and I called the court again, hoping I would get to speak to someone else. The same clerk answered, and when she checked the reference I gave her, she said, 'Did I not speak to you earlier?' I said, 'Yes, but I called again because I thought there had to be some mistake.' I told the clerk I had been told that the hearing had been cancelled. The clerk said, 'Ma'am, there is no mistake. This hearing has never been cancelled. To cancel a hearing, a cancellation request would have had to be submitted in writing.' That made perfect sense to me, because Elizabeth had told Zavier that she had cancelled the hearing on the phone that same day they had spoken.

It was all lies. Elizabeth was scheming to have me arrested. That is why, weeks before the hearing, she had gone quiet on me. And no one else in the family was calling, because they all knew about the plan. They did not check for the one person who plans above all of their plans– my Jehovah-Jireh, my provider.

I turned up for court the next morning – just my Lord and me. When I did not see Elizabeth, I still thought it was all a big mistake. I was jumping for joy in my spirit, because I honestly thought that Elizabeth had indeed cancelled the hearing, and I still thought the clerk had made a mistake. My mind was racing, all kinds of thoughts going through my head. Surely no one could be that wicked, at least not my mother. Surely even Elizabeth could not be this wicked? The thoughts were just racing through my head like horses on a merry-go-round. Each moment that passed that I did not see her or any member of my family, I thought, *See? She is not coming.* I was called in first, and I was seated. Then I heard Elizabeth's name being called. I nearly passed out when, bold as brass, Elizabeth walked in with her head held high, not daring to look at me. I wanted the earth to open and swallow me up at that point in time. I was so devastated to see Elizabeth. I felt faint; I was dripping with perspiration. I simply could not believe it!

I know you are probably thinking how stupid I was for believing that Elizabeth would not show up after all that I had already been through with her. But when all is said and done, she was my mother, and I still loved her. The love that a child has for a mother is an unbreakable one. No matter how cruel and mean my mother had been to me throughout my whole life, I simply could not help it. I still loved my mother. When it was our turn to speak, because Elizabeth was the petitioner, she spoke first. I was so sad to see her actions towards me. This was the first time Elizabeth looked at me, as she pointed at me and said in such an aggressive voice, 'That woman, Your Honour, forced me to sign papers for her house.' In one breath she was saying it was her house, but in the very next breath, she was saying I had made her sign papers for *my* house.

When it was my turn to speak, I said, very calmly and quietly, 'Your Honour, my mother …' The judge was drinking some water, and he nearly choked as I said 'my mother'. He raised his hand as a signal to me to stop. He composed himself as he asked me, 'Ms King, did you say your mother?' I said, 'Yes, sir.' And he said, 'Ms King, tell me why your mother would take you to court today.' I explained to the judge about the house, and how Elizabeth had kept the insurance money and shared it with her children, and would not give me the money to fix up my house.

When the judge heard what had taken place, he threw the case out of court. He said, 'No domestic violence took place here. This lady does not have a malicious bone in her body.' Elizabeth started to speak, 'Bu—bu—, Your Honor.' And the judge said, 'If you don't like my ruling, take it up somewhere else.'

When I went outside, I saw my niece and my brother Luke and other family members. They all left with their tails between their legs. You see, they didn't know about the God that I serve! They had just seen me in that courtroom. I wish God had opened their eyes and shown them all the angels that He had sent to accompany me to court that day.

Finally, it was official. It was my house despite Elizabeth's best efforts to steal it from me. The house was still in Elizabeth's name, and I needed her to sign the quitclaim deed so I could transfer the house over into my name. I got the paperwork and gave it to her to sign, but true to form, she refused to sign my house over to me. Actually, she ripped up the documents!

I still needed to get my house fixed. Luke still had quite a lot of my money, which Elizabeth had given to him, and I needed it back. He had already spent it, but he offered to do some work to compensate for this. I did not want him anywhere near my house again. I was trying to find a worker who was licensed, and Luke said he had a friend who was licensed to do the work. I asked Luke for his information, as I wanted to do some research on this person for myself. I did not trust Luke. Luke gave me his number, so I decided to go onto the council's website where all licensed workers are registered. Search as I might, I could not find this man's details. I had asked to see this man's details when I met him, and he had conveniently left his registration details at home. Really! Did he think I was born yesterday? I was not about to have an unlicensed contractor working in my house. The worst thing was, and I don't know why this should have surprised me, I found out that my brother had cooked it up with this man to charge me four times what the job was worth so they could split the proceeds. I was done with him.

Because I got back less than half the money that the insurance company had sent to do the work, I was having difficulties finding anyone to do the work. I did not quite know what to do, and all the time I was paying the mortgage on the house. I had to make a decision and fast. If Elizabeth wanted my house so badly, I would give it to her. She refused to sign the papers to transfer the house over to me, so let her keep my house! I could buy another house. So for the next two months I did not pay the mortgage. After all, why should I pay if Elizabeth was going to keep on insisting it was her house? Surely she should pay the mortgage for her own house!

I started looking for a place to rent in the interim. After going through these experiences with my family, my faith in God had increased immensely, and I felt a closeness to God that I had not felt before in my entire life. It was at this time, whilst looking for a place to rent, that I had a dream. In the dream, the Lord told me to get out of the house by the fourteenth of the month. I found a place to rent, and I moved out of the house on the seventh. I went back to the house about four days later to pick up some things that I had forgotten in the shed. To my surprise, Elizabeth had gone to the house and changed the locks on the doors. She thought my stuff was still in the house! Again, she did not know about the God that I serve. He always kept me one step ahead of her. Her wicked plot was to lock all my stuff in the house, so I would have to negotiate with her about getting it all back. She was trying to make me pay the mortgage on the house. That did not work, so what now? I mailed the keys for the house to Elizabeth by recorded delivery.

THE SEPARATION

WHEN I MOVED AWAY FROM that house, I swore I wanted nothing more to do with any member of my family except for Zavier. They were just pure evil. For most of the years of my life, I have lived amongst total strangers, and no stranger ever did to me anything like what my family did to me. A conversation I had with my real estate agent, Sean, put it all into perspective. I had not heard from him for months, and when I finally spoke to him, he said, 'Semone, can I ask you a question?' I said, 'Sure, go ahead.' He said 'Are you sure that's your mother?' That was a really good question. Sean was explaining to me just how devastated he was about what my mother had done to me. Even the girls in his office, when they heard, were in tears, because they had worked so hard to get me into that house. Did my brother James know something I didn't when he ran away saying, 'That's not my mom!'

Once I moved away, I kept in touch only with Zavier. He and I talked often, and if he did not hear from me, he would surely track me down.

MY CHURCH

WHEN ETHAN TURNED SEVENTEEN AND graduated high school, he decided that he wanted to go back home to England. After all that he had been through, he just could not deal with the people in our family anymore. There was no loyalty. He desperately missed his brothers and his dad. Oh, my heart was bleeding. I knew I had to let him go, but he was my baby, and he was still so young. Still, I knew I had to allow him to find his way in this cruel world. Oh, I wished I could have kept him with me and shielded him forever, but I knew this was not practical. I had to allow him to make his mistakes and learn from them. It was one of the hardest things I ever had to do in my entire life, but I had to let Ethan go.

Ethan returned to England to finish up his education. The plan was that he would go to university and get a part-time job whilst living with Phil Junior, who had a four-bedroom house. Ethan was very independent, and very soon he took his driving test and passed it. I was very proud of him, and to show him just how proud I was, I bought him a car. He was over the moon. He was working, and he was going to university doing a fashion design course. Ethan was very creative and very good with his hands, so this was really good for him. He studied and worked hard, and soon he was able to afford a place of his own. I was so proud of him. He was young, but he had a wise head on his young shoulders.

After Ethan left, however, I felt an emptiness and a loneliness that I had never experienced before. Just then a friend invited me to a church service one Friday night. I went with her, and I felt that the bishop was speaking just to me. I felt as if there was no one else in that room. I hung on to his every word. From that night until the time I left Orlando, that was my church. I took up my membership, and I stayed there for eight years. I had found a church that I liked, where I could feel the presence of God.

Was this a perfect church? Maybe not for everyone, but it was the perfect church for me. As my bishop would say, 'If you find a perfect church, don't go there, because you will make it imperfect!' This church did so much for me. I learnt so much from my bishop – my doctor, my daddy, as I called him. He taught me self-worth. He taught me my worth as a queen. He taught me that I am 'the catch', not the other way around. He taught me to love myself. Ouch! That's the biggie! He taught me how to look in the mirror and encourage my own self. He taught me that I did not need to wait on anyone to encourage me. He taught me that I am somebody, and most of all, he taught me that Jesus loves me. Jesus will always have by back, my front, and my sides. Above all else, he taught me how to really seek God's face and not His hands.

Going to prayers at 5.30 in the morning was very challenging for me at first, but the benefits far outweighed the lack of sleep. For example, one time the Lord appeared to me in a dream, and all I heard was, 'Pray for your son'. I said, 'Lord, which one? I have three.' So I immediately got up, and I went to early-morning prayers. I started interceding for my three sons.

It was early Sunday morning when I got a call from Timothy. Phil Junior, Timothy, and their cousin Charles had gone on a night out to celebrate Phil Junior's birthday. As Phil Junior and Charles were going to be drinking, Timothy was the nominated driver. They were driving back in the early hours of Sunday morning. Timothy was overtaking a lorry. As he was doing so, in his 3 Series BMW, the lorry driver swerved and clipped the side of Timothy's car. This sent Timothy's car spinning into the central reservation, and Timothy found himself facing oncoming traffic. Meanwhile, the lorry had jack-knifed and was now lying across all six lanes of the busy motorway. At the same time, two bikers approached. Unfortunately, they did not see the lorry across their path in time; sadly those two young men lost their lives in the accident.

Timothy was treated like a criminal and was blamed for the accident, which clearly was not his fault. The lorry driver was unhurt. He came to Timothy after the accident and apologized to him and told him he had been momentarily distracted as his gear stick had slipped out and he had been looking down trying to get it back in gear. This was when he had clipped Timothy's car.

Had it not been for the Lord on their side, both my boys would be dead today. That's the power of having a relationship with God and knowing God for myself, so that when He spoke, I knew how to listen and to intercede for my children. Just about fifteen minutes before the accident happened, Timothy had dropped off their cousin Charles. If Charles had been in the car at the time of the accident, he would be dead today, because he'd been sitting in the backseat, and the back of the car was crushed like a can of sardines. The emergency workers could not believe that my two boys were able to walk away from that accident unscathed. The power of 5.30 a.m. prayers!

My bishop also taught me how to tithe. I had never known the importance of tithing before. I learnt how to give God His 10 percent and more – much more – and not to rob God. When things got hard, I learnt how to stay on my knees. Oh yes, I call being on my knees being in 'Knee City'. There were times when I would fall asleep on my knees praying, asking God for answers to my problems. I have had the privilege of seeing people healed from different forms of cancer, and had I not been there and seen this with my own two eyes, I would never have believed it.

It was in this ministry that I met a young lady, Sharon. Sharon introduced me to her Uncle Simon, who was unmarried, and we started talking. Simon seemed like such a gentleman. He would open doors for me. He spoke to me so gently. He treated me like the queen that I am. Not wanting to walk out of the will of God, and to do things in decency and in order, I introduced Simon to my bishop. My bishop gave us his blessing at the appropriate time to get married. Simon attended church with me every Sunday. What was important to me in a husband, first and foremost, was that he had to love the Lord, and he also had to know God for himself. I felt that, if an individual knew and loved the Lord for himself or herself, then he or she

147

would know how to treat a person in the right way. Simon seemed to have all these qualities.

The first thing that attracted me to Simon was that, one evening, we were talking on the phone, and Simon said, 'Can I ask you a question please?' And I said, 'Sure, go ahead.' To my surprise, Simon asked if he could pray with me. I welcomed this. It was so nice to hear Simon praying for me. Whenever we would talk of an evening, Simon would always close our conversation with a prayer. Simon and I had a short courtship during which he proposed and I accepted his proposal.

Simon and I decided on a quiet wedding at home; I had already had a big wedding before. I had a huge garden, so I hired caterers and decorators, and they did an absolutely fantastic job on the day. I invited Zavier to come and be my give-away father. I gave him strict instructions not to tell Elizabeth or any other members of the family. I should have known better. Zavier is so family orientated.

On the day of my wedding, I got back from the beauty salon, and as I opened my front door, I saw something that completely surprised me. Elizabeth and my sister Hyacinth were standing there along with Hyacinth's daughter. I was so angry, but I gave them each a hug. I went straight to my bedroom, and that's where I stayed until it was time for me to get married.

I had left the wedding co-ordinator at the house, and also the catering and the decorating staff, so the wedding co-ordinator had let my unwelcome visitors in. I was not happy with Zavier, but I refused to let them spoil my beautiful wedding day. I was incensed when it was time to take photos. They were the first ones in my pictures – all smiles. They were so hypocritical! I was incensed. In one picture the photographer caught Elizabeth holding up my hand and looking at my two-and-a-half-carat diamond engagement ring and my wedding band. I was not even aware of this on the day. It wasn't until I saw the photographs that I noticed that.

Simon and I got married in a beautiful ceremony performed by my bishop. We set off on our honeymoon, and when we got back, I moved in with Simon. He already had a house of his own, and as I was renting at the time, it made sense that I would move into his house. It was strange living and sharing a bed with a man again. Since Phil, I had not been interested. I had wanted to give myself time to get over Phil properly so that when I started a new relationship, I would not bring any baggage with me. I figured eight years was long enough.

Simon and I got along so well. We did not argue; we talked a lot. Sometimes we would just switch off the TV and sit there and talk. Communication is a vital part of any good relationship. Simon was also a great cook, and he liked to pamper me by cooking me delicious meals at times. Other times, we would just light up the grill, and we would get a bottle of wine and just cook outside and eat and talk. This relationship was so different from my relationship with Phil. Simon would wake up every morning, and he would say, 'Good morning, Mrs Smith' He would tell me that he loved me, and throughout the day he would say, 'Mrs Smith, have I told you today that I love you?' It was a beautiful relationship at first. Simon and I would talk on the phone during lunchtime, and he would always end the conversation with, 'Mi amor' That was his code, when he was in company, to tell me that he loved me.

The first cracks began to appear after six months. Simon had lived on his own for some time before we met, as his marriage of twenty-five years had also ended in divorce. He got married again straight away on the rebound, and this marriage lasted only two years, which was not surprising given the circumstances.

I noticed that when Simon ate snacks like crackers, bread, cake, or other crumbly foods, he would not use a plate or a napkin. As a result, I could actually use the trail of crumbs to see where he'd been throughout the house. This was not good, especially in Florida, as insects such as ants and cockroaches loved these snacks! Trying to be diplomatic, one day as he was doing this, I said, 'Honey, would you mind getting a plate or a napkin please. To avoid the crumbs on the floor.'

All of a sudden, Simon flipped out. He started yelling, 'Who do you think you are talking to? Do you think I'm a [f ... beep ... beep] boy?' As he continued his barrage of cursing and insults, I did not say a word, because I was stunned. How had my simple and nice request for Simon to get a plate or napkin produced that reaction? I looked at Simon, and his eyes were like those of the devil himself. At that moment, I did not recognize Simon. He raised his hand as if he wanted to hit me, and I just stood there and looked at him. I said, 'Satan, I rebuke you in the name of Jesus! I plead the blood of Jesus against you.' When I said that, Simon literally ran from my presence.

Later on that evening, Simon came to me and apologized. He broke down crying, and said it would never happen again. I had been surprised to hear Simon cursing, because he specifically told me before we got married that he did not curse. He even gave me an example of a friend he once had. They used to play dominoes together, and because of his friend's habitual cursing, Simon had refused to play dominoes with him anymore. As it was early in our marriage, I decided to forgive him, put this behind us, and start again.

Simon was made redundant from his job shortly after that incident, but he seemed to have no desire to look for another job. Every day I would go out to work, and he was quite content to sit at home. I did not like this, and discussed the situation with Simon. His response was, 'I have you now.' I chose to ignore that comment, because I thought maybe I was taking it out of context, but it bothered me.

As the months passed I realized that I had not taken his remark out of context, as all the bills became my responsibility, including his mortgage. I then took on a second job, and still Simon would not go out to work. One day, I came home at lunchtime, as I had forgotten something at home. To my dismay, I found Simon fast asleep in bed. This really got my back up, because whilst I was out there working hard, he was asleep in bed in the middle of the day! He was not contributing to anything in the house. I even paid for his haircuts.

I also noticed that, since we got married, Simon had started making excuses not to go to church. When the excuses failed, he would start picking arguments with me, always on a Friday or Saturday, and he would draw it out until Sunday and would refuse to go to church. I called him out on it, and when he realized I knew what he was doing, we would leave for church together. He would drop me off right by the door of the church and tell me he was going to park the car. Simon would then go back home and skip praise and worship without telling me. I would notice he was nowhere to be seen when I would look around, as I was on ushering duty. This went on for quite a while. Simon would try his very best to avoid being involved in any activities at church.

This was of great concern to me, because Simon's behaviour at home was getting considerably worse where I was concerned. He was becoming very controlling. He monitored my every move. He expected me to go to work and not make any stops. I was supposed to come straight home. He would refuse to eat out, because all of a sudden, he did not like restaurants, but the moment I brought home a take-away, he would be the first one to eat it. When we were court-ing, we ate out all the time, and he did not seem to have any prob-lems doing so. He got so controlling that, whenever my sons called me from England, he would get upset. He would start sulking and separate himself from me by either stomping off to sit in his man's den or going outside into the garden. He seemed to have a problem the moment the phone rang. He just did not want me speaking to anyone – not my friends, not anyone. He even had a problem if I spoke to our bishop!

It got to the point that, whenever I went out shopping, spend-ing my hard-earned money, I would hide the shopping in my car and wait until he was not at home to unload it. The only time I did not have to hide the shopping was when I shopped for Simon. Then he would not have a problem. I could not let Simon know even if I was going out with my friend Rosie, whom he knew very well. I would park my car in a car park and meet up with Rosie, then I would retrieve my car and drive home.

I hated the fact that I had to behave like this in my marriage, but Simon wanted me to have no friends, and at that point, I was simply trying to keep the peace. My youngest son, Ethan, was com-ing to visit us for Thanksgiving. I had not seen Ethan for two years, and I was so excited to see him. When Ethan came, he bought a present for Simon, and they seemed to be okay. However, Simon came to me and said that Ethan had to be in by nine o'clock every night. I told Simon that he was being unreasonable, as Ethan was an adult and he was also on vacation. Simon objected to Ethan driving my car. Why should he? This was my car not his. When Simon and I met, I had my car and he had his car, so why should he object that my son was driving my car?

We had friends around for Thanksgiving dinner, and Simon raised an open discussion about Ethan having to be home by nine, which I thought was totally inappropriate. Our friends were very bewildered that Simon was requesting this of Ethan, and they told him straight that he was being unreasonable. Only at this stage did Simon back down and say that Ethan could come home when he wanted to as long as he did not make a noise to wake him when he got home. Ethan did not have a problem with that. As a matter of fact, Ethan would take off his shoes before he came into the house. Not once throughout his fourteen-day stay did he wake Simon when he got home.

One night when Ethan went out, I decided to go to bed, as I was tired. Usually Simon and I would retire together, but this partic-ular night Simon decided he wanted to watch TV in the living room even though we had a TV in the bedroom. So I left him and went to bed. I got up about three hours later to go to the bathroom, and I saw Simon sitting in the sofa drinking a cup of coffee and having a bit of cake. I went back to bed, and about five minutes later, my cell phone rang. It was Ethan. He said, 'Mom, I'm trying to open the front door, but it's double locked, and I can't get in.' I thought this was strange, because we never double locked the door, and besides Simon was right there sitting on the sofa by the door, so he would have seen Ethan pull up in the driveway, and he would have heard him trying to get in. I got up to let Ethan in, and sure enough, the door was double locked.

What I saw sent a chill down my spine. I saw Simon hiding in the kitchen still with his cup in his hand. Not only had he switched off the TV, he had switched off all the lights in the house. The house was in total darkness. Simon had seen Ethan pull up and decided to lock him out of the house. How malicious! He did not bank on Ethan calling my cell phone. Wow! I did not say a word to Simon.

I simply looked at him, opened the door for Ethan, and went back to bed.

I did not find Simon to be his usual self when Ethan was there; he would separate himself from us. When I wanted to take Ethan out to dinner, I would of course invite my husband. He would decline, but when we got home, Simon would have an attitude towards me. He would sulk and sit in his man's den and just generally be uncooperative. I observed this and noted it.

It was during this time that Simon approached me and told me that I would have to choose between him and my son. I looked at him, and I told him the love I had for my son was different from the love I had for him. I told Simon that I had enough love for both Ethan and him. I also told Simon, 'Don't ever ask me to choose between you and my son again, because you will always lose. My son was part of my life way before I knew you, and he'll be there afterwards. That's a no-brainer.' Simon never ever mentioned that to me again.

As soon as Ethan left, Simon was all over me being his usual self. I did not understand this. We were in the second year of our marriage, and my eldest son, Phil Junior, decided to come and visit us for Christmas with my little granddaughter, Cherish. By this time, I had not seen them in nearly two years, and Cherish had grown so much. The last time I had seen Cherish, she had been only five months old!

Simon was much nicer to Phil than he had been to Ethan. He took Phil out and showed him around Orlando. He absolutely adored Cherish, and Cherish adored him. I even caught him sneaking Cherish ice cream. They got along like a house on fire. I was quite pleased at Simon's progress. Simon, however, still would not look for a job, and this was causing me to lose respect for him. I could not understand how a man could sit back and allow his wife to go out to work – and not even seem bothered!

Simon was a builder, so when he worked, he would earn way more than I did. He would do the odd job here and there, but he got these jobs only by recommendation by word of mouth, or if another builder friend needed help on a job. These jobs were not regular enough to produce a steady income, so we struggled on just my salary. This went on pretty much all throughout our marriage.

Having spoken to Simon for long periods of time earlier on in our marriage, I had learnt a lot more about him than I had known at first. It was during one such discussion that I learnt that he had bought a gun when his ex-wife had left him. He had told me how he had planned to use that gun to kill her when she was leaving work late at night. Simon told me how he planned to back her into a corner and take her out! Simon said that he'd had a change of heart, and he had not gone through with the plan. I did not make Simon any wiser, but at this point, I was terrified because, I thought, surely if he had planned to do something like that to his ex-wife, then, if the occasion arose, he would consider doing the same thing to me.

I mentally recorded these things, as I had to protect myself should anything happen later on in our marriage. One morning I had a day off work, and Simon and I had a late breakfast. We sat there just talking for over two hours. It felt good once again being the way we had been earlier on in our marriage. It was a good morning, or so I thought. I had some things to do around the house, and Simon was outside gardening. I was in the bedroom just doing a general spring clean, and I heard that voice again telling me to look out the window. I went to our bedroom window, and as I looked out into our back garden I saw Simon. He had dragged the new garden sofa I had recently purchased outside, and he was smashing it on the ground. No sooner had he done so, than he calmly picked it up and put it back inside as if nothing happened.

In view of our earlier conversation, in which Simon had told me how he had intended to murder his ex-wife, I was very shaken by his action. I heard that voice again saying to me, 'How long before that sofa becomes you?' I knew then it was time to get out of this marriage. I did not let Simon know that I had seen him break the sofa. Weeks later we were sitting on the patio, and I was sitting on that sofa. I said, 'Oh, this is broken!' I was hoping that Simon would come clean. He held his head down and never said a word, so I said, 'Simon, I saw what you did with the sofa. I saw you break it.' He started crying, and again apologized and said he didn't know why he had done it. That was the confirmation that I needed to get out of that marriage. But how? When? I was sure that, when the time was right, the Lord would reveal it to me.

Several months later, we were coming up once again on Thanksgiving. My middle son, Timothy, would be coming over to see us. Timothy came bearing gifts for Simon as well, and they got on absolutely fine. As he had done with Phil Junior, Simon took Timothy around and showed him a bit of Orlando. Simon also took Timothy to meet his aunt who was ninety-three years old at the time. In fact, Simon and Timothy got along so well that Simon felt comfortable enough to borrow money from Timothy and to ask him not to tell me. However, one of our dinner guests, whom Simon knew very well, had a daughter the same age as Timothy.

This friend's daughter, Sarah, a nurse, thought it would be a good idea to take Timothy out and show him a bit of Orlando. She thought it would be good for Timothy to have a friend his own age to have a bit of fun with. I thought it was very nice of her to offer to do that for Timothy. One evening Sarah called to say she wanted to take Timothy out, but she was just leaving work and she was really hungry. Timothy asked if it was okay for her to eat at our house, as we had plenty of leftovers from dinner. I said sure; I did not have a problem with that. I asked Simon, and he said okay.

I went into our bedroom. Simon was there, and he started cursing, saying some real nasty words. I could not understand why. He started saying that Sarah was coming over to his house too late. I said it would only be seven o'clock when she got here, and she would not be there for long, as all she was going to do was have some dinner, then she would be leaving with Timothy. But he continued cursing at me.

Now Timothy heard the whole thing, and he came to Simon and said, 'Did you just swear at my mom?' Simon did not answer him, so Timothy repeated himself. He asked Simon again, 'Did you just swear at my mom?' All of a sudden, Simon started cursing at Timothy, using the most disgusting words. He put his face in Timothy's face and pushed up his chest. He was actually squaring up to Timothy to fight him! Timothy looked at him and said, 'Don't be silly, Simon. I'm twice your size and half your age!' This did not stop Simon from continuing his abuse. I then got between them, because this was madness. I was not going to see my husband and my son fighting. That was crazy. (You see, during all the years I had been married to Timothy's dad, he had never – not once – sworn at me. Neither had I sworn at him.)

This was a culture shock for my son. None of my children was used to seeing behaviour like this in a relationship. Phil and I never ever argued in front of our children, let alone curse. Timothy said, 'Mom, I'm not leaving you here with this man. I saw something in his eyes that I did not like.' I knew exactly what Timothy was talking about, and for me this was confirmation yet again that I needed to get out of this marriage. That very night, Timothy and I left the house. We went and stayed with friends. We actually stayed with Sean, the real estate agent, Rosie's son.

The next day we went back to the house to pack up some of my things. When Simon saw Timothy, his first words were, 'Get out of my house!' He went and picked up a cricket bat. At this stage, I called the police, because all I wanted was to pack a few necessary things and leave. The police came. A female police officer said, 'Mrs ..., I came out here some years ago on a domestic violence call. Was that for you?' I said, 'No ma'am, that was not me.' I found out later that that call had been for Simon's ex-wife. The officer asked me, 'Did you not know about this before you got married?' I said, 'No, ma'am.' She was about to take Simon to jail, but Timothy and I begged her not to, so long as he allowed us to pack my things. Simon agreed to this, and the officer told him that, if she got another call, he would be going to jail. Simon was as good as gold. He did not bother us again the whole time we were there packing my stuff.

Only when Timothy knew that I was out of the house and staying with friends did he return to England. What a vacation! I found a place of my own a month later, so I went back to the house with a moving van and movers and moved the rest of my belongings out of Simon's house. He kept on asking me where I was moving to, but I never told him. He then decided to play the only card he had left which was, 'You are my wife. I have a right to know where you are.' No way was I going to make that mistake and give Simon my address. I remembered what he had said about the gun. I did not know if he still had that gun. I had never seen it in the house, but he could easily get another if he so desired.

Simon kept on calling my phone and telling me he wanted us to get back together. I told him I would do that under three conditions: One, he would get to know the Lord again. Two, he would get a steady job. And three, he would get counselling. Until he did all of those things, we would remain apart. Simon agreed to do all three things, but a year went by and he had not committed to doing any of them. He was still calling me and telling me that he wanted us to get back together. He told me how much he loved and missed me. Sure he missed me – he missed the luxury of being at home and not having to work, and having all his bills paid!

I decided that I had given Simon enough time to take action, and he had proved to me that he was either not capable of doing so, or he did not want to, so I decided to change my phone number. To date, I have not spoken to Simon. I have initiated divorce proceedings. I believe Simon was a very nice man at some point, but I blame myself for the breakup of my marriage, because I did not take enough time to really get to know him. I believe I got married to Simon too soon. I believe that, had I waited and gotten to know Simon better, I would have seen the warning signs. I say that, but I have to say that Simon was a very good actor who fooled all of my friends and family members, so how long he could have kept on pretending I don't know. So it may be that, even if I had taken another year to get to know him, he would have continued to be deceptive, because he'd had so much practice at it. It's hard to know if I would have seen the signs, but only time would have told!

When I married Simon, Zavier had taken it upon himself to let my family have my telephone number. And they knew where I lived – ever so briefly, as I was moving after the wedding, thank God. Elizabeth or my sister Hyacinth would call me and invite me to different functions. I did not take them up on any of their invitations. After three years, they started asking why I never attended anything they invited me to, so I decided, being a good Christian lady, I could no longer live in the past, and I needed to let bygones be bygones. So, ever so slowly, I began attending probably one out of six functions my family invited me to. Then I increased this to perhaps two out of six, and so on.

I always made sure I could make a quick getaway just in case of trouble. Somehow, I just still did not trust them, because I still got the feeling that, given a chance to do what they had done to me in the past, if the opportunity arose again, they would do something similar in a heartbeat. I would not allow this to happen – once bitten, twice shy.

It was around this period that I got a phone call from Zavier. He was in Jamaica vacationing with his family. By this time, my older brother, James, had relocated back to Jamaica after the death of his father. I had not spoken to James in many years. When I was leaving England for America, I looked for James to let him know that I was leaving. I was very saddened when I arrived at what had been James's father's home. The building had been completely renovated. I hardly recognized the place. I rang the doorbell, but strangers answered the door. I asked a few questions as to the whereabouts of the family that had lived there, but this family had no details. I was heartbroken. I went to the other property that I knew belonged to James Senior, and I got the same response. I had lost touch with James, and I had no way of contacting him. It wasn't until I spoke to Zavier, after I arrived in the United States, that he told me that James was now living back in Jamaica. I had asked Zavier for James's number, and I actually called him, but it was the wrong number. I told Zavier that I had tried to call James, and he told me James had changed his number and he would let me have the new number at a later date, as he was driving and was unable to retrieve it from his phone.

I had planned on calling James, but alas, it was not meant to be. There is an old saying: never put off for tomorrow what you can do today. In this case, unfortunately, I should have pushed Zavier for the number instead of waiting until another day. When Zavier went to see James when he was vacationing in Jamaica, he was given the news that James had just passed away that very morning. James died suddenly from a heart attack; he was only fifty-six years old. I was devastated. I felt as if we had unfinished business.

Elizabeth called me and told me that she would not be attending the funeral. I was furious, and I decided to sit down and speak to her about the consequences of her actions. I told Elizabeth that, regardless of the fact that she had not seen or spoken to her son in over thirty years, James was still her firstborn child, and she owed it to James to pay her last respects. I told her that, if she did not pay her last respects, then she would live in regret for the rest of her life. As usual, she had to consult with her other children before taking my advice. Later on that day, Elizabeth called me to say that Hyacinth and the rest of her children were in agreement with what I had told her, so she would attend the funeral. I never saw any tears shed by Elizabeth for my brother James. Elizabeth just behaved as if everything was normal. You would never know that James was her firstborn child. Luckily, James's real family spared no expense to ensure that James got a good burial. Elizabeth, of course, contributed nothing to her first child's funeral.

Elizabeth and my other family members had done things to me that I might have expected, to a certain degree, from strangers. But I would never have expected that level of meanness, jealousy, and hatred from my own relatives. I have heard it said that the ones who are closest to you are the ones who can hurt you the most, and that's very true. It happens because your guard is down, because there is a certain level of trust and a certain level of expectancy. You don't expect your mother to lie on you or to your sisters and brothers and poison their minds against you. You don't expect your mother to steal your house. You don't expect your mother to go to court and lie against you, and make up a charge against you that you did not commit. You don't expect your mother to scheme to get you arrested. You don't expect your mother to lie against her own grandchild, whom she had not seen in fifteen years. You just don't expect your own mother to steal from you. All of these things you would expect from a stranger – and I mean not from a stranger who is a so-called friend, but from someone who does not know you. But you certainly do not expect this from your own mother!

After leaving Simon, I rented a beautiful three-bedroom house with a lovely swimming pool and huge front and back gardens. It was a house that I really liked, and the alarm system meant that I felt very safe and comfortable there. Although I was living only half an hour's drive away from Simon, this house was so far away from the main roads, that, unless you had specific business down that road, there would be no need to travel there. Actually, that was one of the things that had attracted me to that house. I also had a private land-lady, which was important to me, because it meant that my name would not show up anywhere as owning or renting a house. It was crucial to me that Simon had no way of finding out where I lived. As it turned out, I was living only ten minutes away from Hyacinth, but I did not let her know that for quite a while. I had to be careful, and even when I did let her know where I lived, I did not tell any of my family that Simon and I had broken up. I wanted them to think that I was not alone.

Again, my life was about to take a turn I could never have predicted.

Ethan was getting restless in England and felt that he needed a change in scenery. I suggested he come over for a while, as I still had his bedroom set up, and I did have a three-bedroom house, so there was always plenty of room for my children when they came over to visit. Ethan decided to come over, and I just loved having him there. It was fantastic. He had a job set up, and he could drop me off at work and drive my car when he needed to until he was ready to buy his own car.

After a few months however, the job turned out not to be at all how it had sounded in the beginning. Ethan worked as instructed, but was not paid for a whole month. This had a domino effect, as Ethan had been borrowing money from me during that period. We felt it would all even out when he finally got his pay. I did not have much money myself, and the money that I had been lending Ethan was my rent money. And I had leant it only on the basis that he would get it all back in a few days. A few days turned into a few months. I was in sales, and at that time of the year, January, things were very slow. I did not get paid a salary; I worked on a commission-only basis.

Before I knew it, I was a month behind in my rent, but I was still not too bothered, because I was still waiting on Ethan to get paid so he could repay me. By this time, I had been in the house a year and four months and had never been late with my rent. I called the landlady and explained to her why she had not received the rent, and she was very trusting and said she would wait for it.

Three months went by, and still Ethan had not been paid. I told him I could not afford to keep putting gas in my car for him to go to a job for which he was not being paid, despite the fact that he was going to work every day. I was making a little money – enough to pay our bills and buy food – but certainly not enough to pay the rent. This was turning into a nightmare situation. At this same time, my work permit expired, and although the lawyers were dealing with the situation, immigration was dragging their feet, and I could not work without a work permit.

Here I was with a good job that I was unable to do. I had no money coming in, and Ethan was in a situation in which he had no job and no money coming in.

I'm a firm believer that God places people in your life to help you through certain situations, and this was certainly true of a few people I will mention. The first person was my beloved bishop. By now I had been going to this church for seven years, and had never asked for a single thing. All I had ever done was give and give and give – much of it sacrificially. Even after much fasting and praying about the rent situation, I still, because I had so much pride, just could not bring myself to even call my bishop to ask him for help. I spoke with a friend, Sasha, who had told me on numerous occasions to ask my bishop, but I had not done so. Sasha said, 'I need you to hang up the phone now, and call your bishop and ask him to help with your rent.' I said, 'Okay, I'll do it.'

With tears in my eyes, I still could not bring myself to call my bishop. Instead, I sent him a text to ask if he was able to help with my rent. Without any hesitation, he texted me back immediately and asked how much I owed. I told him, and he texted me back: 'Come to the church tomorrow and pick up a cheque.' I was overwhelmed. I could not believe that someone would ever do that for me. God is an awesome God.

My friend Rosie, whom I had met through The Circle and with whom I spoke on a daily basis, had also introduced me, by phone, to a lovely gentleman whose name was John. I had been talking to John for eight years, and we had become really good friends. John and I never met in person, but we talked at least every week, and sometimes every day, depending on our schedules. I told John about the situation I was in. As far as I was concerned, I was just talking to a friend and not expecting anything. I was just grateful I had some-one to listen to me, as I was very stressed at the time. I did not even ask John to help. The next day I received a text message from John telling me that he had sent me some money by Western Union. I was shocked, as I was not expecting that. John had not just sent me the money to pay my rent, but had sent me more than enough money to be able to buy food for Ethan and me as well. I was now truly begin-ning to learn who my friends really were.

I would truly see, in the difficult months ahead of me, just how valuable John was to me as a friend. I have never in my whole entire life come across someone with a heart that was even better that my heart. I love that man. Whenever possible, John would send me money to get me through some difficult situations. He was truly God sent. He gave so much, and yet he never asked anything of me. What a gentleman! To date I have still never met John, but I hope one day we will put faces to the names. What a friend! My bishop has always said, 'He wants ride or die folks around him.' And I truly know from this experience with John exactly what he meant. Imagine, I had never ever met John. All we had ever done was speak on the phone for the past eight years. I did not even know what this man looked like, and here he was sending me money for my rent and food.

Compare this, if you will, to the attitude of my family. They knew I was in trouble, because I could not work, and they never once offered to help. They were secretly gloating that I was having prob-lems. At this time, I was so broke I was going to food banks to pick up food so that Ethan and I could have something to eat. The food that we were picking up from the food banks was mostly outdated food, but we were desperate, and when you are in a desperate situation, you take drastic measures. There were times when I would buy a rotisserie chicken from my favourite food club. It was precooked and only cost $5. I did this on several occasions, as this would last us for the week. Ethan and I would eat chicken every week for months until we were sick of the sight of it. Ethan would take a fork to pick out whatever meat was left on the bones, and when there was simply no more meat, we would still not throw the bones away. We would boil them to try to make soup, hoping to eek out what little flavour might be left in them. When Ethan and I got so sick of chicken that we simply could not eat it anymore, we had to look for another source of protein that was also cheap to buy, but plentiful, and that would last us the week. We came up with the idea of spareribs. We discovered that we could get a whole box of spareribs for only $12. At first we were quite happy with this, but as we had with the chicken, we soon got sick of eating spareribs. There was no other meat we could afford to buy, so we would alternate between the chicken and the spareribs until we simply could not even afford to buy either of the two.

My sons would help out, but they too had their bills to take care of, and to be fair, I never really told them the extent of our suffering. By this time, I was five months arrears in my rents. I lived in fear every day that we were going to be evicted and thrown out on the streets, but somehow, God in His infinite mercy, kept us in that house.

Whilst I was fighting these battles, my bishop called me one day. He knew that I had a three-bedroom house. There was a young lady in the church by the name of Delvita. Bishop explained that Delvita was homeless, and she needed a place to stay. I knew Delvita very well, and although I enjoyed my privacy, I agreed that Delvita could stay with Ethan and me for a few months.

I know, you're probably thinking I'm crazy considering that Ethan and I did not even have food for ourselves. And to make matters worse, Delvita did not work. I figured that, if God allowed bishop to ask me to accommodate Delvita in this desperate time in my life, then somehow I was meant to help her. I spoke to Ethan, and he felt the same way I did. I told Bishop yes, I would allow Delvita to stay with Ethan and me. I figured, if God had provided for Ethan and me, then surely He would provide for Delvita also.

I went about getting the spare room ready for Delvita. I vacuumed and dusted and put fresh sheets and pillows on the bed. I made the room very welcoming for Delvita. When she arrived, I gave her a tour of the house and told her that we did not have much to give at present, but she was free to help herself to whatever was in my fridge and my cupboards in terms of food. I told her that, in this house, we were family, and I welcomed her into my family.

Ethan and Delvita became very close. He looked up to her as the sister he never had, and I treated her like the daughter I never had. There were times when we were so desperate for money. I remember one time in particular. A well-known fast-food restaurant was selling ice cream cones at a reduced rate of only 50 cents. One night we were all so desperate for an ice cream that I went all through my house searching for every cent that I could find. Between the three of us, we managed to find $1.50, and we went to the drive-through. We were too embarrassed to go inside. We bought three fifty-cent ice cream cones. We felt as if we had won the lottery. That ice cream was the best ice cream I had ever eaten. Or at least that's how it felt.

Everything Ethan and I had we shared with Delvita. It was such a positive experience having her live with us at this time. Ethan and I certainly learnt a lot from her. During that time, I learnt about fasting, and most importantly I learnt about a place called 'Knee City'. I was on my knees morning, noon, and night. One of the demands I placed on God was, 'Lord, I paid my tithes and offerings faithfully, and you said in your word, 'I have never seen the righteous forsaken or their children begging bread' (Psalm 37:25 New International Version). I reminded the Lord how I had sowed faithfully in His house, and God certainly honoured the seeds I had sown.

When I was working I had never withheld my tithes and offerings. I was faithful to God, and in turn God was faithful to me and my household. The word of God says, '"Bring the whole tithe into the storehouse, that there may be food in my house. Test me in this," says the Lord Almighty, "and see if I will not throw open the flood-gates of heaven and pour out so much blessing that you will not have room enough for it"' (Malachi 3:10 New International Version).

I know that only the grace of God could have kept Ethan and I in that house, and that is exactly what happened. We stayed in that house until we – and the keyword here is *we* – were ready to leave, and I never hid from the landlady. I explained to her my situation, and she just trusted me to do the right thing by her. She restored my faith in human nature, because she could have easily thrown us out on the street, but she didn't. She worked with us in every way possible, and I am grateful to God for Kim. She showed me that she was interested in me as a person, and not just as the provider of the rent money. All this time, I was still waiting for immigration to renew my work permit.

Despite what I have been through in my life, I have learnt never to allow a situation to make me bitter; rather, I allow every situation I go through to make me better. I have also learnt that everything we go through in life is not necessarily for us; often it is to help someone else along the way. I am hoping that readers of this book will be inspired and know that God is truly real.

Sometimes in my life I have asked, *Where is God? Why has God forsaken me?* Sometimes I have thought, *Why is God mad at me?* I have come to the realization that those were the times when God was mad *about* me and not *at* me. Something would always happen unexpectedly, and that something would be exactly what I needed at the time. Without the Lord on my side, I never would have made it through the hell that I have been through. But to God be all the glory. I have been through hell and back in my life, but today, this book serves as my testimony that I am still standing by the grace of God. I realize that I had to go through what I went through, because if I had not, I would not have been able to write this book to encourage others along the way.

EPILOGUE

GOD HAS BROUGHT ME FULL circle in my life. The same house that I shared with Phil, which as you will recall, was sold to Phil Junior, is the same house I am now sharing with my son, Phil Junior, and my two beautiful granddaughters, Cherish and Precious. It is from this home that the Lord inspired me to write this book.

I am every woman:

I've been homeless, and He provided for me.

I've been hungry, and He gave me bread to eat.

I've been poor, but He made me rich.

I've been afraid, and He comforted me.

I've been in darkness, and He provided light.

I've been sick, and He healed my body.

I've been in despair, but He gave me hope.

I've been weary and oh so tired, so weak, but He gave me the strength that I needed to carry on.

There were times when I didn't think I could make it, but He gave me his grace and His mercy.

I've been in situations in which I could not see a way out, but He made a way for me. Jesus is the way maker.

All I have needed Thy hands hath provided! 'Great is Thy Faithfulness'- (Thomas Chisholm)

God is no respecter of persons. He did it for me. He brought me through some tough times, and He will surely do it for you also!

www.ingramcontent.com/pod-product-compliance
Lightning Source LLC
Chambersburg PA
CBHW071359120626
46546CB00002B/752